"Faithful to the radical gospel itself. Stands as a prophetic, honest, highly useful reminder of what the gospel is." —*Malcolm Boyd, in* Christian Century

"A genuine understanding of the parables of Jesus." —*Charles G. Hamilton, in* The Churchman

"Challenging and just controversial enough to be an excellent jumping-off place for lively discussion groups—for either teenagers or adults." —*Ruth S. Smith, in* Church and Synagogue Libraries

"Calls for radical commitment to Jesus' understanding of 'The God Movement.' " —*Leander E. Keck, in* Religious Studies Review

"Biblical reflection on the radical gospel demands of faithfulness to the kingdom of God. For anyone concerned that our religion, our wealth, and our culture have imprisoned us." —*James B. Olson, in* The Circle

"Jesus' parables of the kingdom come alive through imaginative paraphrase, careful analysis, and searing application." —The Other Side

"Captures the spirit of the Gospels so well that I would like to buy a hundred copies of it and stuff all my friends' Christmas stockings with it." —*Jack Dick, in* The Catholic Weekly

"A good introduction to the pungent 'biblical radicalism' of Jordan." —Sojourners

Cotton Patch
Parables of Liberation

Cotton Patch
Parables of Liberation

25th Anniversary Edition

Clarence Jordan and Bill Lane Doulos

A Koinonia Publication

Herald
Press

Scottdale, Pennsylvania
Waterloo, Ontario

Library of Congress Cataloging-in-Publication Data
Jordan, Clarence.
    Cotton patch parables of liberation / Clarence Jordan and
Bill Lane Doulos.—25th anniversary ed.
      p. cm.
Includes bibliographical references.
ISBN 0-8361-9151-X (alk. paper)
1. Jesus Christ—Parables. I. Doulos, Bill Lane, 1943-
    II. Title.
BT375.3 .J67 2001
226.8'05209—dc21   00-143891

Scripture credits and copyright clearance information appear on page 8.

*In memory of
Clarence and Florence Jordan*

Scripture Credits and Copyright Clearance Information

Contents

Foreword by Jim Wallis 11
Preface 13
Introduction 17

1. Shattering the Status Quo 21
2. Overcoming Old Allegiance 25
3. Reaching Out for Liberation 35
4. God Against the Church! 46
5. God Against the Rich! 60
6. Disturbing the Peace 71
7. Children of Arrogance 86
8. Children of Grace 94
9. Counting the Cost 105
10. Trade with These Ideas 114
11. The Works of Mercy 126
12. The Parabolic Life 139

Notes 149
The Authors 153

Foreword

In my study, above the desk where I write, is a wall full of pictures. They're photos of people who have inspired or nurtured me over the years. Whenever I write anything, they are peering down at me to help guard what I say.

One of those people is Clarence Jordan, whose commitment to the gospel led him to establish an interracial farm and community in rural Georgia long before the civil rights movement even began. This "Koinonia" was a radical example of Christian living. in starkest contrast with its surrounding culture.

Though hardly an academic, Clarence was also a powerful biblical scholar and teacher. His Cotton Patch Version of the New Testament, placing the ancient writings into the U.S. Southern context, is moving, enlightening, and entertaining—all at once. Clarence had a way of retelling the biblical text that was unique and made people sit up and notice.

Good preachers know that the most effective way of making a point is to tell a story. Our main role model in that is Jesus himself. The parables recorded in the Gospels are some of his clearest and most compelling teachings.

Cotton Patch Parables of Liberation is a faithful rendering of those stories, placed in a modern context and idiom. Using stories from his native South, Jordan gives exciting new life to old parables.

Jesus' stories are particularly devoted to explaining

the "kingdom of God"—Jordan's favorite concept—
with a call to discipleship and to liberation from all
that imprisons us. But to respond to this call, we have
to leave old ways of living for a new and at times
unknown existence, just as when God called Abraham
to leave his home and journey to a new land.

Jesus, and Jordan, call us to leave our comfortable
existence and begin a pilgrimage to the kingdom. In
their new setting, the modern parables recover what
must have been the startling impact on the original
hearers. They question, confront, and challenge. They
are urgent and dramatic. They show us old truths, but
in new ways.

When this book was published twenty-five years
ago, our review in *Sojourners* called it "a good introduction to the pungent 'biblical radicalism' of Jordan."
That observation remains true today.

For those who have never met Clarence Jordan, this
book is a good introduction. For those who have read
him in the past, it is a good reminder of his wisdom
and eloquence.

As my old friend Bill Lane Doulos notes, "You have
a choice: put these parables on the shelf and return to
your civilized existence, or prepare yourself as best
you can for a rough ride."

I commend to you the ride, and I thank Bill and
Herald Press for once again bringing this book to our
attention.

—*Jim Wallis, Editor-in-Chief of* Sojourners
Washington, D.C.

Preface

In many respects, the people of Koinonia created this book. *Koinonia* is a Greek word meaning fellowship or community. It is also the proper name for a group of Jesus' followers who have resided for various time periods on a farm near Americus, Georgia. Clarence and Florence Jordan and a few others founded Koinonia in 1942. It is an attempt to demonstrate the kingdom of God in the midst of an alien world.

The proclamation, teaching, and application of the gospel have engaged Koinonia in expanding ministries:

• Conducting discipleship schools.

• Building houses and selling them to poor families in southwest Georgia, at cost and without interest charges.

• Running a farm, food processing, sewing, and craft industries that provide jobs for the unemployed and profits for a Fund for Humanity.

• Publishing and distributing books and records that communicate the radical ideas of Jesus Christ.

• Operating a preschool development center for neighborhood children.

Throughout its diverse history, Koinonia has consistently witnessed to three central gospel ideas: peace, sharing, and living as brothers and sisters.[1]

Clarence died at the farm in fall 1969.[1] For over a

quarter century, he had provided a major share of the spirit and the muscle that gave birth to Koinonia.

As a Greek scholar and a farmer, Clarence divided his working time between the fields and the books. He translated most of the New Testament into the Cotton Patch Version of the ancient texts. This is a twentieth-century rendition, with a southern flavor.

Many of Clarence's lectures were taped and have provided the material for records and a book, *The Substance of Faith and Other Cotton Patch Sermons.*[2]

This present volume includes most of Clarence's teaching on the parables. Clarence spoke before a variety of audiences, and often without notes. In my editing, I have tried to retain the freshness of his spoken communication.

Clarence helped to build and inspire Koinonia; just as surely, Koinonia helped to produce the incisive style and content of Clarence's speaking and teaching. During the various months I spent at the farm, spread over several years, the Koinonia people have stimulated me. All of them, past and present, have contributed to this book because they have nurtured my own spiritual growth. While at Koinonia, I accepted the name "Doulos" (servant).

Several have assisted in specific ways through their encouragement and suggestions. Among these, I owe particular thanks to Ladon Sheats, Al Zook, Suzanne Phillips, Florence Jordan, Larry Hesed, Erika Walton, Carolyn Mosley, and Sybil Doulos.

I have attempted to weave together the thoughts of Clarence and myself with excerpts from his Cotton Patch Version (except where otherwise noted).

Clarence's commentary is set apart from my own framework by the sanserif Optima type, as first flagged on page 22. His translations, indented as extracts, are followed by the New Testament references. My own contribution is in the Palatino type that you see here.

In this twenty-fifth anniversary edition, I have fine-tuned the text to stress how inclusive the gospel is, and how God is our Father and Mother, our heavenly Parent. I am confident that this is in the spirit of Jesus Christ and of Clarence. I hope the reader is able to view this book as an organic whole.

Despite the extensive guidance of Clarence's writings, the worthy inspiration of the fellowship at Koinonia, and suggestions of those individuals listed above, I assume final responsibility for the message and accuracy of the book.

—*Bill Lane Doulos*
  Koinonia Farm, Americus, Georgia, and
  All Saints Church, Pasadena

Introduction

The parables of Jesus lead us into the kingdom of God. They come to us where we are, make use of things and feelings familiar to us, transport us into an unfamiliar realm of values and relationships, and invite us to make ourselves at home.

For example, Jesus spoke of a man who found a buried treasure. Jesus might have been imagining a tenant farmer out working the owner's field when the plow struck a metal chest. This was common in Palestine; centuries of invasions had forced families to hide their valuables underground. He uncovered the treasure, then buried it again. In his excitement and joy, he went off to sell all his possessions so he'd have enough money to purchase the field.

Jesus said that such hazardous venturing is a good picture of the demands of the kingdom of God. This farmer risked all he previously valued for the sake of his extraordinary find. Wherever the kingdom of God is discovered today, men and women are leaving familiar patterns and pioneering a new existence.

This new existence is what the gospels and particularly the parables are all about. The very possibility of something new is liberating to many. How shall we recognize the treasure, respond to its presence, and permit it to refashion our whole way of living?

Jesus answers these questions by using his favorite teaching medium: *the parable.* This book addresses these same questions for us to face in our day.

In *Cutting Loose: A Civilized Guide for Getting Out of the System,*[1] Dorothy Kalins speaks to executives and their spouses disenchanted with the rat race and routine. People who had been swallowed up by big salaries and social acceptance tell their stories of liberation. They found release in going to the country, beginning modest ventures, doing as they pleased, living simply, and sharing life with their families.

Jesus also invites us to cut loose. When he says, "Follow me," he is talking about a radical change overtaking us. The shortcoming of Kalins's approach hinges on that word *civilized*. Many so-called civilized things can't guide us in getting out of the old system; unredeemed civilization and the worldly system are intertwined, giving birth in turn to one another.

Among many other things, civilization as known from history has always brought war, exploitation, racism, and sexism. What we need to help us cut loose is an "uncivilized" guide. We need to recognize an "uncivilized" Messiah walking toward us with his gift of the kingdom of God, asking us to order our lives anew, along unfamiliar but God-honoring lines.

The kingdom of God is the theme of Jesus' preaching, teaching, and healing. This kingdom is not a low-risk, blue-chip investment created by society for our consumption. It can't be calmly considered and casually digested. God's kingdom can't be domesticated; its leader can't be restrained from his continuous challenge to our selfish way of life.

Jesus' parables bring us something new and wild. In interpreting them, it is not fair for us to make them conform to our old polite ideas about what is good, acceptable, and "civilized." Jesus has his own grasp of what is good and acceptable.

Years ago, I talked to an executive at a large university. He confided that he was disenchanted with his career. I brashly invited him to consider a career in Christian service.

He left me squelched and speechless by the insight of his response: "Why should I leave one rat race just to get into another?" He was familiar with the "Christian service" industry and was looking for a more radical alternative than I could offer at the time. Here it is: *there is nothing more radical than what Jesus offers,* as this book explains.

I used to work for Young Life, a Christian outreach organization that welcomed hundreds of first-time campers to its Colorado ranches each summer. The welcoming speech usually included these words: "For you campers who have never ridden a horse before, we have some good news. We have some horses here that have never been ridden."

In the *Cotton Patch Parables of Liberation,* we have attempted to corral a few of Jesus' parables. Clarence Jordan lends us his earthy translations and imaginative insights. I offer a bit of my own horse sense, the best of which may be summed up as follows: some of these horses have never been ridden.

Therefore, you have a choice: put these parables on the shelf and return to your civilized existence, or prepare yourself as best you can for a rough ride. We may find ourselves landing together in some unpredictable places—and may be pricked by cactus.

1
Shattering the Status Quo

The parables of Jesus help us see two realities: the reality of a world whose values must be rejected, and the reality of a new world whose values must be accepted.

It is easy for us to live in a comfortable culture and to assimilate the values of God's kingdom into a system produced, so the historians tell us, by our Judeo-Christian heritage. The American Jesus comes to us rather tamely, tidies up a few bad habits, makes us better citizens, and sends us back into a "civilization" that is grateful for our good influence.

Everything flows smoothly. Christianity seems warm and right to us. There is no comprehensive discontinuity between what we have been and what we are or shall be. There is no rejection of traditional values; sadly, there also is no entrance into the kingdom of God.

When we try to fit our Christianity into our culture, we are really clobbering a square peg into a round hole. We are trying to mix oil and water. In Jesus' metaphor, we are trying to put new wine into old wineskins. Two parables say best what we must do when we encounter the kingdom—either by accident or after years of searching. These are the twin parables found in Matthew 13:44-46.

The God Movement is like a man finding a treasure buried in a field. He covers it over again, and then with great excitement, he sells all he owns and buys that field. (Matt. 13:44)

Clarence put it like this:

The kingdom of God is like a man plowing in a field. He discovers a treasure, a box. He's plowing with his old ox there. All of a sudden he hits something and thinks it's a rock or a stump. Yet he sees it glitter like metal. He quickly throws his plow aside, scratches around, and finds it is a treasure box.

What does he do? Well, he might say, "You know, this is a wonderful discovery I've got. I think I'll go to school and write a Ph.D. dissertation on treasure-hunting." But this isn't what he does. In his great excitement, this guy has the ability to decide on a clear-cut decisive course of action. He says, "I'm goin' to sell all I've got and buy that field."

He's got a sign up in the classified ads. "For Sale: one house. For Sale: one fiberglass boat. For Sale: this and that." He is goin' out of business. But is he? He's just gettin' ready to go into business. This man knows what he's doin'.

I think a lot of times we don't go into the kingdom business because we just aren't smart businessmen. We want to hold onto our little trinkets. We want to hold onto our status. Oh yeah, we gotta keep our status. We can't be fools for Christ. We can't give up our house.

But this guy is ready to sell out so he can get this treasure of great price. This is the kingdom; this is part of the revolution. To be in the revolution, you many times have to divest yourself of all earthly possessions. You gotta make some adjustments in your standard of living. And Jesus generally calls on people to make adjustments that are downward, not upward.

The God Movement is also like a jeweler looking for special pearls. When he finds a super-duper one, he goes and unloads his whole stock and buys that pearl. (Matt. 13:45-46)

Jesus said the kingdom is like a man seeking goodly pearls. He finally sees one of great price. He goes out, puts up a Going-Out-of-Business sign on his shop, and liquidates all his lesser pearls to get that one of great price. This is a parable showing that the call to the revolution is a drastic one, calling for people to really reshape their lives, their standard of living, their set of values, all the things they had thought were important. Out the door they go, all for the sake of this one great and consuming passion, the revolution that God wants to usher in on this earth.

These parables don't give us the specifics about what must be rejected, and they don't tell us the precise content of the new discovery. They do tell us that the discovery is so overwhelming that it shatters routines characteristic of our old way of living. The discovery can't be assimilated without major change. Business can't go on as usual. *Jesus is talking about transformation, not mere reform.*

Two questions confront anyone who is serious about discipleship.

1. *Have I discovered the treasure?*

Chances are that the treasure is close—perhaps even familiar. We are like children playing with dynamite. Our problem is that we don't know what we're holding. We're in danger of spending our lives going to church, reading the Bible, saying our prayers, doing a few good deeds, being baptized and buried—all without being startled by the great discovery! Listen closely for the clink of the blade against the box.

2. *Has the treasure reshaped my life?*

Perhaps we really have made the discovery. Now the stakes are higher for us. We know that we cannot afford to be casual. Our energies and imaginations have been fired by a new affection. Is it conceivable that we might let the super pearl slip through our fingers? That we might go on plowing until our excitement cools and our memory fades? That the status quo might survive?

2
Overcoming Old Allegiance

Once Jesus talked about the varying responses to the kingdom of God. His conclusions are summarized in the parable of the farmer recorded in Matthew 13.

One day Jesus left the house and sat down on the seashore. Such a big crowd gathered around him that he got into a boat and sat down while the people stood on the beach. He told them many *comparisons.*[1]

"One time a farmer went out to plant. As he did so, some of the seeds fell on the path, and the birds came along and gobbled them up. Others fell on rocky places where the soil was shallow. Because they weren't planted deep, they came up right away; but not having a deep root, they withered when the hot sun hit them. Still others fell among the weeds, which grew up and choked them out. But others fell on good dirt and matured, some multiplying a hundred times, some sixty, and some thirty. Now please let *that* soak in." (Matt. 13:1-9)

Matthew unravels this parable for us as follows: Many hear the message of the revolution and do not catch on because the evil one comes and snatches away what has been planted in their hearts. These are the wayside seeds. The seed planted on the rocky and shallow soil refers to those who, when they hear the message, right away get all

25

hepped up about it. But they do not have any roots within because they're wishy-washy. They soon get tripped up.

Other seed fell among the weeds; people heard and received the message, but then the cares of this age and the deceitfulness of wealth choke out the idea, and it becomes fruitless.

The ones who are the deep earth, however, hear the message, understand it, and bring forth abundant fruit. This is the parable of responses; in each instance the same idea or seed was planted. But the results were different.

Sometimes we preach to people and give them the Word. We read it to them from the Greek and the English—Phillips, King James, Revised Standard, and New English Bibles—yet they don't get it. It just goes in one ear and out the other, with nothing in between to stop it.

The people come in where they can hear the sermon. As the preacher stands at the door, they shake his hand and tell him what a fine sermon it was that they slept through. That's the end of it. They're goin' about their business. The message just never makes any contact; it never fires up anything. They're just there.

Then there are all those people who listen. You've got a crusade for Christ, you know, and you've got people listening and singing and getting all hepped up. Everybody comes down to the front and makes a profession of faith in Christ. "Oh, ain't it wonderful!" But then, when the sailing gets rough, and when persecution arises because of the Word—"Well, nobody made it clear we were gonna get persecuted. They just told us we were gonna get a free ticket to heaven. What do you mean, gettin' persecuted? That wasn't part of the contract." These are the shallow people.

Next, there are those people who represent the good dirt,

but they're preoccupied with other things. They're fine people, and good-hearted. They mean well. But they're just cut off from ever realizing their potential by the rat race, or whatever kind of race people are puttin' on now. The cares of the world, the distractions of this age, and the deceitfulness of riches (perhaps riches are the most deceitful of all things)— these things just choke them out and prevent them from ever maturing.

Now it seems to me that this really classifies modern-day Christianity more than anything else. By and large, I think, Christians are good people. They're nice, middle-class, suburban people. They're well educated; they mean well. They don't hate Jesus! In fact, they love him, if he'll stay in his place. They don't mean him any harm. It's just that they're so busy.

They've got to go here; they've got to go there. They're busy with their houses, they're busy with their automobiles, they're busy with their business. They just don't have time to think, and they don't have time to get on the ball. So they're choked out.

But there are those who do bring forth fruit, some a hundredfold, some sixty, and some thirty.

Here again, Jesus is hitting upon the truth that is so difficult for us to grasp, no matter how many times it's said and no matter how many ways it's phrased. The gospels are pointing a finger directly at us and saying words we don't want to hear: "Response to the kingdom means rejection of the traditional values that have shaped our lives."

We have been victimized by three attitudes that this parable lays bare. We may be like the seed upon the hard path, stripped of our capacity for growth and reduced to a short and meaningless existence. We have learned how to remain aloof. There is no room for response to anything new. We are amoral robots, programmed by our culture to go about our business without emotion, and without the slightest possibility of making any delightful discoveries.

Some of us, represented by the shallow soil, are seemingly the opposite, but the end result is the same. We have the capacity for immediate and impulsive response to the kingdom, but the fear of unknown consequences reveals that we, too, are robots. We don't have the stamina for the long haul or the perseverance for the hard times. We let ourselves be dehumanized by persecution.

Finally, some of us are naive at the point of Jesus' greatest concern. We are duped into thinking we can maintain a foothold of respectability in both worlds. We naively suppose that material wealth and spiritual wealth can coexist. We want to embrace the values of two worlds because we don't understand that those two worlds are on a collision course.

The amazing truth of this parable is that the sowing of God's ideas does create obedient discipleship. Some do genuinely respond. The truth penetrates our hardness, overcomes our fears, and destroys our old allegiance. The kingdom takes root in our lives and brings forth an abundance of faithfulness.

I remember breezing along the Pennsylvania Turnpike a few years back. The status quo for me at that time was about 70 miles per hour. I passed many signs that said that 65 was the maximum, but they made no impression. Then I came to a larger billboard portraying a fist with a forefinger pointing squarely in my direction. The caption in letters several feet high read, YOU, SLOW DOWN.

My foot instinctively went to the brake for fear this hand was literally going to reach out and grab me. I had been seeing those speed-limit signs, but they weren't registering. If they had sunk in, not being a foolish or reckless person, I would have slowed down. But the Pennsylvania State Police had to draw me a convincing picture.

So it is with Jesus, trying to shock us awake us with the reality of our situation, and with the crucial nature of the opportunity confronting us. He comes to us in parables because we tend to look without seeing and to listen without hearing or catching on. In connection with this use of parables, Matthew quotes a passage from Isaiah;[2] it also applies to us:

> They strain their ears and never catch on;
> For the hearts of these people are hard,
> And their ears are dull,
> And their eyes are dim.
> Otherwise, their eyes might see,
> And their ears might hear,
> And their hearts might understand,
> And they might turn around,
> And I'll make them well. (Matt. 13:14-15)

Jesus draws us pictures; he stages little dramas for us because he wants to make us well. But there seems to be something in us that doesn't want us to understand. We apparently want to hold to the death-dealing systems that Jesus has come to smash.

These systems may impose upon us a job, an income level, a social milieu, or a lifestyle that keeps us enslaved to its own preservation. At the same time, it keeps us too busy to accept an invitation to a greater feast, one that Jesus talked about in Luke 14:

> One time a man gave a big dinner, and he sent invitations to many people. When everything was on the table, he sent his servant around to all the guests, saying, "Y'all come; it's all ready."
>
> But one after another began to beg off. The first one said, "I have bought a tract of land, and I've just got to go and look it over. If you will, please excuse me." Another said, "I have bought five teams of mules, and I simply must go and try them out. If you will, please excuse me." Another said, "I just got married, and therefore I cannot come!" So the servant returned and told his boss what had happened.
>
> Then the boss had a fit. He said to his servant, "Run out real quick into the streets and alleys of the city, and bring in here the poor and the disabled and the blind and the crippled." After a while his servant announced, "Sir, I've done what you told me, but the table still isn't full."
>
> The boss then said to the servant, "Well, go out on the highway and sidewalks and collar them to come on in here, so I'll have a full table. Because I'm telling you a fact, not one of those guys who got an invitation will get a taste of my food." (Luke 14:16-24)

Jesus was trying to show that the kingdom of the new order, this family of the Father, is like a big family gathered around the table, eating together. It's fellowship. It's fun. It's feasting. It's joy. It's life. It's beauty. But a tragedy is also involved. Some people choose not to attend. Here Jesus' picture of going to hell was not about a place of torment, but about being left out of the joy of the fellowship.

Jesus began, "There was a certain man who made a great supper, a big banquet." Now we know that this man represents God. God made a big banquet, and that's the kingdom, and he invited a lot of folks. He sent his slave out, at the hour of the supper, and he said to those who had been invited, "Y'all come; it's all ready."

They, beginning with the very first one, began to beg off. The first one said, "I have bought me a farm, and I've got to go and look it over. I beg you, please have me excused."

Now this fellow rejects the invitation by saying, "I'd like to come to your banquet. I know you're going to have some mighty good stuff. I heard about that barbecue you make, and it's very, very nice, and I'd like to be there for it. But I bought me a piece of land."

This word *land* was a powerful idea to the Jews. To buy a piece of the Holy Land meant to be a part of a nation of people. The people and the land were, somehow, tied up together. You really had a corner on God if you had a little piece of God's land that you could own. Every devout Jew wanted to own—even if it was just a few square inches—a bit of his native soil. This, I think, was Jesus' way of symbolizing nationalism and patriotism.

So this fellow is saying, "Well, I want to come, but I don't agree with this idea of yours that you let anybody in there, no matter where they're from. We've got to think of the kingdom in terms of America. America is for the Americans, you know. We can't let these other folks be part of the inheritance. So I'm going to hold onto my little piece of land. I've got to look it over." Super patriotism! It keeps people out of the boundless kingdom of the Spirit.

Then another one said to him, "I have bought me five yoke of oxen, and I've got to go and try them out. I beg you, will you please have me excused?" Now this is an interesting kind of thing: "I have bought me five teams of mules," we might say. In Jesus' day, folks didn't have a two-car garage, but many had at least one yoke of oxen.

The yoke of oxen was a detachable power unit. You could hook 'em up by day and plow with 'em, and then hook 'em up to the cart at night and go courting with 'em. It was a combination of jeep and tractor, a power unit to which you could attach various implements.

Nearly every family had at least one yoke of oxen. Some rich folks out in the suburbs even had two. But here's a guy who's got five yoke of oxen! What's he doing with so many jeeps? I don't know, but unless I miss my guess, this old fellow was a used ox dealer.

He'd been to the auction and bought him several yoke of them. He had them over in the barn, polishing up their toenails, grooming up their horns, combing their tails, and getting them all ready to put out in the showroom the next day. That's what he was going to do with them.

This man was all business, a freewheeling, free-enterprise, capitalistic businessman. He said, "Sure, I'd like to go along with you in this enterprise, but I've got to make some money. I've got to open up early in the morning there.

"I belong to the Ox Associates. We've got chains of ox dealers all over this country. They transferred me. I'm area supervisor of the ox dealers in this section here, and if the corporation told me to go to Timbuktu on an ox deal, I'd go over there."

The other man said, "I have married a woman; therefore, I can't come." He just said "therefore." It wasn't any use to ask to be excused. He was told to be home by six o'clock. He wasn't going to that banquet.

Now what does this man represent? He is simply saying, "I'm not going to break with my wife." She is the symbol of all family relationships. My wife is the symbol of all the social ties, rising above friends, above relatives, and even above families.

He is saying, "I just don't want to belong to a movement that's going to break up my family, that's going to put me at odds with my parents and my brothers and sisters. I admire the movement, and I think it's got some good things, but I just don't feel that I can sacrifice my friends and my relatives for my convictions. I'm just honestly going to tell you so. I can't be there."

The slave came back and reported all these refusals to his lord. The master was angry and said to his slave, "Well, run out quickly to the streets and alleys of the city, and bring in here the poor folks, and the crippled, and the lame, and the blind."

His servant went out and gathered them all together, and he came back and said, "Master, what you told me to do has been done, and there's still some room around the table."

The master responded to the slave, "Well, then, run out to the country, get the country folks, and bring them in here, so that my house might be full. I want to tell you," he added, "not one of those guys who was invited shall eat of my supper."

In this parable we have a description of what the kingdom is, what keeps us out, and the dangers of refusing our opportunity to participate. Old allegiance must fall if we are to give an adequate response to God's invitation to his big banquet, the kingdom of God.

3
Reaching Out for Liberation

We're beginning to get the picture: Jesus is using these parables to shake us loose, to get us to open our eyes. There are things in our lives that we have always thought were good ingredients for kingdom citizenship. We participate in some time-honored social structures, we might even say some "sacred" institutions. God takes his proper place alongside family, country, and occupation.

But what if God is demanding more than what we count as his proper place? What do we do when God loses his civility, when he withdraws his blessing from middle-class American values? What happens when we must choose *between* God and social relationships, *between* God and country, *between* God and mammon?

There is no doubt that these choices come to us. The parable of the great feast is reaching out to grab us. If we think the decision is not urgent, we are wrong.

One parable in particular emphasizes the critical nature of taking immediate action in view of impending circumstances. This is a crisis parable. The text itself is in Luke 12:58-59, but it is particularly helpful to quote the context beginning at verse 49.

> I came to kindle a fire on the earth, and what wouldn't I give if it were already roaring! I have an ordeal to go through, and how pressed I am until it comes to a head! Do you all think that I came to give

the world peace? No, I tell you, not peace but conflict. From now on, if a house has five people in it, they shall be fighting—three against two, and two against three. A father will be against his son, and the son against his father; a mother against her daughter, and the daughter against her mother; a mother-in-law against the bride, and the bride against her mother-in-law."

He said to the crowd, "When you see a cloud blowing in from the west, right away you say, 'Here comes a rain,' and sure enough, it does rain. And when the south wind is blowing you say, 'It's gonna be hot,' and hot it is.

"You phonies, you're skilled at weighing scientific facts, but how is it that you can't interpret the signs of the times? And why can't you tell what's right for you? For example, when you're going to court with a man, wouldn't it be better to make an effort to settle out of court rather than having him drag you before the judge, and the judge rule against you, and deliver you into the custody of the warden, and the warden slap you into the pen? I'm telling you, you won't get out of there till you've paid through the nose." (Luke 12:49-59)

We seldom think of Jesus as coming to kindle a fire on earth, to bring conflict. Yet wherever Jesus went, he seemed to precipitate awkward situations and often crisis situations. The upshot of his ministry was crucifixion. Jesus passes the crisis on to us, and he asks, "Why can't you tell what's right for you?" What's right for us is (1) to recognize the crisis, the fire that is about to consume us, the imprisonment that is about to rob us of our freedom, and (2) to respond before it is too late.

We are in a crisis, and we must act swiftly; that is the virtue of the man on his way to court. He is able to perceive that his time has come, that his freedom must be seized by immediate action, or lost. There is no more breathing room.

He has maintained the semblance of freedom, but now judgment is about to fall on him.[1] He has nurtured the naive hope that some evidence would turn up to acquit him. But now he must take an extraordinary step: he must strike a last-minute bargain with his accuser. Far better for him to swallow his pride than to lose his freedom.

This parable is designed to impress upon us one thing: the urgent need for decisive action. The kingdom of God is upon us. Our liberation is at stake.

The truth of our own situation is that we too are on our way to prison each time we reject the overtures of the kingdom. If we do not understand that a fire has been kindled, if we have not been electrified by what's happening in our lives and in our world, then we have accepted a personal destiny that cannot liberate us. We are experiencing a fake freedom; but all the doors that lead to life, to joy, to a fearless quest for wholeness for ourselves and our world—all these doors are being bolted shut by our apathy and fear.

To enter the kingdom is not to enter a restrictive network of do's and don'ts. It is to escape such confinement for the sake of a limitless expanse of spiritual abundance.

Sometimes we are more afraid of what freedom *might* mean for us than of what bondage *does* mean for us. The status quo and the old allegiance are the bread and water we are tempted to accept as our regular prison fare—unless the truth of our circumstances and of God's calling can get through to us, and unless we act decisively upon that truth. "The truth will liberate you" if you are an "honest follower" of truth.[2]

The remainder of this book will be concerned with "truth" and with "following" where Jesus, through his parables, leads us.

Why all this talk of crisis? Of urgency? Of the need for immediate action? Why do we need to recognize incompatibility between who we are and who God is asking us to be? We must remember now that we are trying to see the parables simply and clearly. To do this, we must try the best we can to leave behind our presuppositions about what is normal Christian experience.

The parables are not innocent and neutral stories designed for our momentary amusement or to confirm a commonsense approach to spiritual development. This is not "story time" but "life-changing time."

We need to recognize the parables as an integral part of the total life and teaching of Jesus. It is clear that Jesus was a revolutionary. We do not have space to lay out the massive evidence supporting this contention, other than to point out the obvious: Jesus was crucified. Storytellers don't usually get crucified. Yet it was a parable that led Jesus right to the brink of ruin.[3]

If anyone is rocking the boat, we hope it is Jesus. We should not be surprised, if we are to judge by his past behavior patterns, that Jesus is once again shattering the pretense of good religious folk.

We have difficulty with the ideas of urgency and discontinuity. We are much more at home with slow, contemplative processes of gradual reform. We tend to see Jesus as the source of a broad, generous, and accommodating invitation to come along into the kingdom by a process of osmosis rather than metamorphosis.

"Follow me" has lost its abrasive ring. But in reality, much to our dismay, the Gospels speak of kingdom entry as a "narrow" proposition. Simple familiarity with Jesus does not qualify one for admission.

Clarence gives us the following translation and commentary on Luke 13:22-30.[4]

Now Jesus was going along from city to city and preaching in the villages, making his journey to Jerusalem. Then somebody said to him, "Lord, are just a few being rescued?"

And he said to them, "You put all you've got into entering through the narrow gate, because many, I tell you, will do their utmost to get in but just won't make the grade."

Then he told this story: "When the householder has gotten up and locked the door, then those on the outside will begin to stand and knock at the door, saying, 'Master, open up for us.' And then he will answer and say to them, 'I don't know where you come from.' Then they will begin to say, 'Well, we ate with you, and we drank with you, and you taught up and down in our streets. And then he will say, 'I just don't recognize you at all. Get away from me, you religious gangsters.'

"Out there (on the outside), there will be weeping and

grinding of teeth, when you will see Abraham and Isaac and Jacob and all the prophets in the family of the Father, but you, yourselves, will be cast out. They will come from the east and west and from the north and south, and they will gather around the table in the family of the Father. And I want to tell you that those who are on the bottom will be on top, and those who are on top will be on the bottom."

I doubt if many of us have seen ourselves as outsiders in terms of the family of the Father. Perhaps we should take another look. On several occasions with his parabolic discourse, Jesus gives us this simple guideline: "Those who are on the bottom will be on top, and those who are on the top will be on the bottom."[5]

Sometimes we wish the parables were more complex and obscure! Taking this statement at face value, it could be a warning to anyone caught reading this volume. People who read religious books may thereby possess some of the trademarks of middle-class religious snobbery.[6]

This warning goes double for people who write books. They show that they are able to spare time from the sheer effort for survival.

There is not enough evidence here to convict you. But if you continue reading, this book may begin to sound like your indictment.

This idea that the last shall be first and the first last is repeated so often in the Gospels that it has become trite and commonplace. But it is a startling truth when we put it into the context of economics, social prestige, military might, and religious elitism.

Jesus did not choose the parables to convey commonplace truth. Quite the opposite. He clothed his most radical ideas in the garb of farmers, merchants, and field hands. The familiarity of the characters in these kingdom dramas disarmed Jesus' audience and set them up for his devastating message.

Clarence explained the procedure this way:

A parable is something you use when the situation is very dangerous. You hide your truth in it; it's a literary Trojan horse. You know what a Trojan horse is. You've read in Greek history of how Helen was captured. She was taken captive into the city of Troy, and all of her kinsmen went out to rescue her. They camped around Troy, where she was held, and they besieged it and they battered it and they couldn't take it.

Finally some fellow had a bright idea. They built a great big ol' wooden horse and sneaked a few men inside of it. Then all the other Greeks went away. When the folks up on the wall of Troy looked out in the morning, they didn't see anybody out there—nothin' but this great big wooden horse. They said, "Well, those guys have just given up and they've gone. But look at the thing they've left."

So they opened up the gates and they all went out there and said, "Well, that's a fine ol' horse. Maybe we could take him into town and build a big merry-go-round to go with him, and we'll just have a wonderful thing." They were looking and looking, but they didn't see anything; they were listening and listening, but they didn't hear anything.

So they got them a jeep and pulled that ol' horse into the city, not knowing what they were doing. You see, the real thing was hidden inside. They weren't aware of what was happening. So they pulled it on past the gates to right where those Greeks had wanted to go all along. They put the horse on exhibit all day, and let school out so the children could see him.

But early the next morning, about two o'clock, when everybody was asleep, the little trapdoor on that horse opened up, and the men came out. They rushed to the gates of the city, opened them up, and by that time, all their soldiers had come 'round. The Greeks came in and took the city.

Now Jesus used that kind of a Trojan-horse technique under certain circumstances. He used it when the situation was dangerous, and when his hearers were difficult. When they would just stop up their ears and shut their eyes, and they wouldn't hear and they wouldn't see, Jesus would bring out a Trojan horse and ram it through their ears and get it beyond their blind eyes.

This wasn't a new technique for Jesus at all. Others had used it. You remember that Nathan the prophet used it on King David.[7] King David was roaming his palace one day and was way up on top of the flat roof. He looked down like a Peeping Tom and saw in the neighboring courtyard a beautiful young lady taking a bath. He asked somebody to please find out her name and telephone number, and they came back and told him that she was Mrs. Uriah the Hittite.

"Oh, Mrs. Uriah the Hittite, huh?" says David. "Bring her to me." You know what happened. After Mrs. Uriah was expecting their child, David tried to hide his sinful use of power by more wrong use of power. He muttered, "Ummm, . . . too bad." Then he told his staff, "Call the local draft board. Have Mr. Uriah classified 1-A and put on the front lines."

Pretty soon there was the inevitable government telegram informing Mrs. Uriah that she was a widow. Then a little later there was a wedding, and King David married the widow.

Now this infuriated Nathan the preacher. He wanted to say something to David about that. If he'd been like John the Baptist and followed the Baptist tradition, things would have gone badly for him. You remember when Herod took his brother's wife, John the Baptist went running in there and said, "What do you mean, taking your brother's wife?" And ol' Herod said, "Put that little Baptist preacher in the clink." So John the Baptist got locked up, you see; he wasn't wise.[8] But Nathan knew he might get put in the jug if he went in with that kind of thing.

So he went to King David one day and said, "King David, I got a little problem."

"What's your problem, Reverend? You buildin' an educational plant and need a little money?"

"No sir, no sir, not that."

"Well then, do you need a new mimeograph machine?"

"No sir, I don't need that. My problem is that I've got two church members who are giving me a little trouble."

Now King David was not suspicious of anything. He didn't know what was going on.

Nathan continued, "I've got two church members giving me a little trouble. One of them is a very rich man with a lot of sheep. And another member of my church is a very poor man, with just one sheep. Well, King David, the rich member had somebody come and visit him. Instead of going out to his flock and getting one of his sheep and killing it to have a little barbecued lamb, he goes and gets the only sheep my poor member's got and kills it for himself."

Now King David got so mad, he said, "Who is that kind of fellow? Show him to me; I'll sure fix him up."

Well, you see, David had pulled the Trojan horse in; he'd pulled it past his gate, on into the inside, and Nathan unlocked the door, pointed at David, and said, "You ask me who the man is? THOU ART THE MAN!"[9]

King David had passed judgment on himself. There wasn't anything he could do then but go out and write another psalm.[10]

Many of the following *comparisons* will be Trojan-horse parables. As you come to understand them, you will find yourself in jeopardy. Perhaps you have already been threatened by the parables of the farmer sowing his crop and of the great feast. Do you identify with one of the three varieties of nonproductive soil? Are you one of the guests who made excuses? Who or what controls *you?*

I now have shared several insights that you might unwisely use to shield yourself from the incisive truth of the parables we are about to consider: Beware of the innocent story. Beware of the Trojan horse. Beware of the easy self-assurance that protests, "But we are the children of Abraham."

This book is not an attempt to entrap you, but to set you free. Our only hope for liberation is to see God as he truly is and to see ourselves as he must see us. If you construct your defenses in advance so that you can duck when the punch of the parable comes your way, then you're the loser. The parables are a means of treading softly until the climactic scene unveils the villains and the heroes.

Sadly, most of my readers, unlike Jesus' audience, are already acquainted with the plot. We already know that the wealthy and the "righteous" turn out to be the bad guys; the Samaritans, tax collectors, and other assorted prodigals turn out to be the good guys. So there is no point in trying to maintain suspense. My only hope is to be straightforward, to plead with you from the beginning to permit yourself to be "set up," to hear "You are the man!" "You are the woman!"

Let us begin with that assumption. Jesus is leveling a shotgun loaded with accusations at many of us. If we acknowledge the truth of our indictment, there is still hope for us as there was for the panic-stricken defendant on his way to court.

Before we consider our hope (below, chap. 8), let us take stock of our predicament. The kingdom of God has come. We have not acted decisively. We have not abandoned our standpat lives. We have striven mightily to maintain our priority power positions over all those more lately coming to the kingdom.

We have not reached out to grasp our freedom. Indeed, if we are honest, the parables we are about to consider reveal that our religion, our wealth, and our culture have been imprisoning us.

4
God Against the Church!

The true children of God are the ones who carry with them the nature of the heavenly Parent. It is impossible, therefore, to separate the parables telling us about God from those speaking about discipleship. As we look at who God is, we pick up essential clues about who we're supposed to be.

One thing needs to be clear: we can't change the character of God, but the nature of a man or a woman can be changed. The possibility of human conversion is an inherent part of the good news. Some of us may be confused at this point. We think the good news is that *God* can be changed so that we can avoid having to change our own lives. But the parables don't give us a choice about who God is; they only give us a choice about who *we* are going to be.

Clarence recounts the following story about the time when Koinonia, the integrated farm community he founded in southern Georgia, was having a good deal of trouble with its "Christian" neighbors. He begins by making the point that membership in God's family is optional, not automatic.

I don't think Jesus taught that everybody was a child of God. He did not teach that *all* men are brothers. He taught that all *could* be brothers and sisters. And he didn't teach that *all* people are children of God. He said all *could* be children of God.[1] Now this is a vital point, because there's so much tommyrot goin' around today about the brotherhood of man.

And there's a lot of tommyrot goin' on about integration. I know the church of God does not respect color lines, but its aim is not integration. People say, "Well, you know, we have to learn to live together here on earth 'cause you know heaven is integrated." Sure, heaven's integrated. Hell is too. They're both integrated. Integration isn't the difference between heaven and hell.

I went to see a Baptist deacon out our way, to see if he would sell us some ground limestone to go on our land. Our land's rather acid; to grow clover or legumes, you have to put about a ton of ground limestone on each acre. We wanted to plant about a hundred acres of clover. So we asked this Baptist deacon who had a limestone agency if he would spread a hundred tons of limestone on our land.

By that time, the violence of the midfifties had subsided. Nobody was shootin' at us or blowin' up our homes. We thought maybe this deacon would like to sell us a little lime.

So he said, "Well, Mr. Jordan, I appreciate your askin' me and offerin' me that business 'n' all like that. But to tell you the truth, I'm scared."

I said, "Well, I'm scared too. But who are you scared of?"

"Well," he said, "I'm scared to tell you who I'm scared of."

"Man, you *are* scared! Well, what are you scared of?"

"I'm scared that if I do business with you, they might blow up my trucks."

I said, "Yeah, I think they might. They are right handy with dynamite. I wouldn't doubt it at all. But in times past, Christians have been called upon to lose not only their businesses, but if need be, their heads."

"Yeah," he said, "I read about that."

"You don't wanna be a part of it?"

"Noooo," he said, "not me!"

"Well, I guess I'll have to be going."

So I started to leave, and he called me back.

He said, "Say, come here. Maybe we can work out some way for you to get that lime."

I thought, here's a Christian who's gonna be a man. He's gonna stand up and be counted. He isn't gonna be one of those kind who withers away when persecution arises. Maybe he's gonna stand up and bear a little fruit. Maybe a hundred tons of lime! I don't know. So I went back in.

He said, "Uh, I think maybe I can sell you that lime if you'll make a public statement that you folks no longer believe in integration, and if you have that statement printed in the *Americus Times Recorder.*" That's our little daily paper.

I said, "Now, my dear friend, we didn't come in here to trade our souls. We came in here to buy lime. But you got us wrong. We never have from the beginning said that we believe in integration."

He said, "What do you believe in?"

"All we've ever said is that God is no respecter of persons, that there's no white and black in the household of God."

"Good God A'mighty, that's integration, ain't it?"

"No sir, that isn't integration," I said. "That's the nature of God. And I don't see any point in us puttin' a little ad in the Americus paper that God ain't what he used to be. In the first place, I don't think God would even see it; he gets the *Atlanta Journal.*

"But assuming that he did see it, I don't think it'd make much impression on him. Looky here. We haven't been able to change even the Supreme Court, and I think God's more bullheaded than those Supreme Court justices. If we can't change the Supreme Court, how do we ever change God?

Maybe we just have to make up our minds to get along with God and just cooperate with him and let him be what he is."

Well, we didn't get our lime. Still haven't got it. But God's still no respecter of persons.

In this book we're going to shelve our attempts to refashion God in our own image. We're going to concentrate on the original God, keeping in the back of our minds the possibility that he hasn't changed much over the past two thousand years.

Three of the most familiar parables reveal to us the essence of this original God. They happen also to be among the most explosive of Jesus' stories. They appear to speak about a sheep, a coin, and two sons, but they really concern the nature of the Father. Clarence gives a full analysis of each story following his translation.

Now all the "nigger-lovers"[2] and black people were gathering around Jesus to listen. And the white church people and Sunday school teachers were raising Cain, saying, "This fellow associates with black people and *eats* with them." So Jesus gave them this comparison:

"Is there a man among you who, if he has a hundred sheep and loses one of them, will not leave the ninety-nine in the pasture and go hunt for the lost one? And when he finds it, he joyfully puts it on his shoulders and goes home with it. He calls over to his friends and neighbors, 'Hey, y'all, I found my lost sheep. Isn't that wonderful?'

"I'm telling you, in the same way there'll be more

joy among the spiritually sensitive ones over a single 'outsider' who reshapes his life than over the ninety-nine 'righteous' people who don't need to change their ways." (Luke 15:1-7)

The whole new order of the Spirit is going to ride on our concept of God. What kind of platform does he have? What does he want to see accomplished? All of Jesus' ethics are rooted deeply in the nature of God. He didn't say, "Love your enemies and give 'em fits." He didn't say, "Love your enemies because that is the best strategy." He said, "Love your enemies that you might be children of your Father."[3] This is the starting point for these parables in Luke 15.

The text says that when this fellow finds his lost sheep, he takes it home with him. He brings that little lost sheep right into the living room and says, "Hey, I got my sheep!" His wife says, "Get that sheep out of my living room. He's going to mess. Get out! I just vacuumed in here!"

Now this is a crazy thing for a man to do with a lost sheep. But he's so happy he's got it that he brings it in, even though it's making a stink. He says, "I want him in my living room. Here's my lost sheep; I've found him."[4]

Do we get the point? Jesus is saying that God Almighty is that kind of God. He goes a bit further and says, "There will be more joy over this outsider than over ninety-nine good church members."

Or suppose a woman has ten pennies[5] and loses one of them; won't she get the flashlight and a broom and sweep and look carefully till she finds it? And when she does find it, she calls over to her friends and neighbors and says, "Hey, y'all, you

know that penny I lost? Well, I found it. Isn't that
nice?" In the same way, I tell you, there's a rejoicing
on the part of faithful ones over a single "outsider"
who reshapes his life. (Luke 15:8-10)

The drachma was the smallest of all coins used in Jesus'
day, like our penny. This woman had ten of them, and she
lost one.

I don't know about all this, but here's what I'm guessing.
I'm guessing that these pennies had a sentimental value.
They were part of a necklace that this lady had. Back in
those days, when you got married, you wouldn't give a
woman a ring—you gave her a necklace to put around her
neck. I would guess that this woman had caught her broom
handle in her wedding necklace and broken it.

The coins just went every which way. She found nine of
them but couldn't find one of them.

It says she lit a lamp, got a broom, and swept and swept
and swept until she found it. She perhaps wore out a fifty-
cent broom for a one-cent piece. Now what kind of economy
is that?

Well, it wasn't the value of the penny. The hero of this
parable is not the penny. All it did was just roll away and get
lost. This isn't a parable of the lost coin; this is the parable of
the sweeping woman. And it isn't so much the actual cash
value of that penny; it's the sentimental value, the love asso-
ciated with it.

My wife's got some chinaware. It's so precious to her
because we got it for our wedding. We set it out when we
have company. On one such occasion, I was doing my chore
of washing dishes, and she said, "Be careful, Honey." I kept
washing, and in a little while I broke a cup. Then everything

got real quiet. Now, I'm used to the storm, but it's the calm before the storm that bothers me. I kinda thought I'd better look around and reconnoiter and see what the situation was. I found my wife in a very sad mood.

"Now listen," I said, "I'll get ya another one; don't take it so hard."

She said, "You can't get any more." They were out of print or out of bake or whatever you call china. "They don't make 'em anymore."

Well, unless I miss my guess, the little ol' cup probably wasn't worth much; it wasn't worth crying over, but it had sentimental value. It was part of a set. And she didn't want the set broken.

I think this is what Jesus is saying about God. Every little human being in this world is part of God's set. God just has a sentimental attachment for his set, for all of humanity. God doesn't go by the kind of arithmetic that you and I go by. He has never learned to deal in fractions. God didn't get that far in school. I think he's like my father, who had ten children. Many a time I thought, "Well, my goodness, with a family this big, Daddy can't love me very much. I can only claim one-tenth of his love." But my father loved me with all of his love. It's just that way with love. There is no fraction in it.

You can't break it up into pieces. And God wants the whole human race. He just can't deal in fractions.

So Jesus is saying to these people who were griping and mumbling and grumbling about the fact that he was taking in all kinds of people, bums and drunks and the poor and everybody. He was saying, "Well, I can't help it. God just has a sentimental attachment for his people. Whether you like it or not, God loves 'em, and it does seem to me that if they're precious in God's sight, they ought to be precious in yours, too."

He went on to say, "A man had two sons. The younger one said to his father, 'Dad, give my share of the business.' So he split up the business between them. Not so long after that, the younger one packed up all his stuff and took off for a foreign land, where he threw his money away, living like a fool.

"Soon he ran out of cash, and on top of that, the country was in a deep depression. So he was really hard up. He finally landed a job with one of the citizens of that country, who sent him into the field to feed *hogs!* He was hungry enough to tank up on the slop the hogs were eating. Nobody was giving him even a handout.

"One day an idea bowled him over. 'A lot of my father's hired hands have more than enough bread to eat, and out here I'm starving in this depression. I'm gonna get up and go to my father and say, "Dad, I've sinned against God and am no longer fit to be called your son—just make me one of your hired hands." '

"So he got up and came to his father. While he was some distance down the road, his father saw him and was moved to tears. He ran to him and hugged him and kissed him and kissed him.

"The boy said, 'Dad, I've sinned against God and you, and I'm not fit to be your son anymore. . . .' But the father said to his servants, 'You all run quick and get the best suit you can find and put it on him. Get his family ring for his hand and some dress shoes for his feet. Then I want you to bring that stall-fed steer and butcher it. Let's all eat and whoop it up, because this son of mine was given up for dead, and he's still alive; he was lost and is now found.' And they began to whoop it up.

"But his older son was out in the field. When he came in and got almost home, he heard the music and the dancing, and he called one of the little boys and asked him what in the world was going on. The little boy said, 'Why, your brother has come home, and your daddy has butchered the stall-fed steer, because he got him back safe and sound.' At this, the older brother blew his top and wouldn't go in.

"His father went out and pleaded with him. But he answered his father, 'Look here, all these years I've slaved for you, and never once went contrary to your orders. And yet, at no time have you ever given me so much as a baby goat with which to pitch a party for my friends. But when this son of yours—who has squandered the business on whores—comes home, you butcher for him the stall-fed steer.'

"But the father told him, 'My boy, my dear boy, you are with me all the time, and what's mine is yours. But I just can't *help* getting happy and whooping it up, because *this brother of yours* was dead and is alive; he was lost and has been found.'" (Luke 15:11-32)

In those days, a young son could ask for his share of the inheritance before his father died. This was not an unusual kind of thing. If the boy wanted to take his money and go off to school, he could do it, or if he wanted to take his bit of money and set himself up in business, he was not making an unusual or unique request of his father. This was his privilege. But if he asked for such a division of the estate, then he had no more legal claim. He could not come back later and say, "Well, how 'bout taking me back in?" It was a cutting of the ties, once and for all.

So this young fellow went into a far country, and there he wasted his inheritance, living like a fool. When he came to his senses, he returned home. His daddy saw him a long way off and welcomed him back into the family.

Now the older boy was out on the back forty when all this was going on. He was plowing the cotton and the peanuts with his old mule. The day had been hot, and the sun was beating down on him. The mule had been slow, and the gnats and horseflies were about to wear him out. He was having it rough and beginning to think seriously about a call to the ministry. Down our way, they have a saying: "A slow mule and a hot sun have called many a man into the ministry."

So this older son decides to call it a day. Coming in from the fields, he sees the house all lit up. He sees one of the barn boys standing outside.

"Hey, what's going on in there? What's all the lights on for? What's all the music?"

The little boy says, "Ain't you heard? Where have you been all day? Your brother's come home."

"My what?"

"Your brother!"

"I ain't got no brother. He's dead."

"No, your daddy said he was dead, but now he's alive. He's come home."

"Yeah, and I'll bet Pa took him out to the woodshed and . . ."

"No. He said, 'Go get a suit for him and a ring. Put some shoes on his feet. And get the fatted calf and barbecue it.'"

"Pa said that?"

"Yeah."

"After he'd already given him half the estate, he goes and gives him all that too?"

"Yeah. That's what he did."

Then the old boy goes into the barn, puts his mule in, kicks him in the belly, sits down on a big of bale of hay, and starts to pout. His daddy goes out there and says, "Son, come on in here and get your plate of barbecue."

"I ain't gonna eat no barbecue."

"What's your trouble?"

"Listen here, Pa. All these years I've been here, I've been a perfect son of yours. If you said, 'Plow peanuts,' I plowed peanuts. If you said, 'Chop cotton,' I chopped cotton. I went with you to church. I got a badge for ten years of perfect attendance. I've been a good boy here, and I just don't understand how it could be that when this, your son, comes home, after wasting your money and living with harlots, you kill the fat calf for him."

Now where did all this business about harlots come in? Up to this point, nobody said anything about harlots. The storyteller just said that this younger boy had wasted his money living like a fool; that didn't necessarily mean he was running around with women.

But this older boy thought that his brother was doing what he would have been doing, if he had been out on his own. He just gave himself away. By judging his brother, he passed judgment on himself. Here is the real prodigal, the one who stayed at home. He was mentally wasting his substance in living with those harlots. Every time he went down the peanut row, he was thinking about one of them.

The father reminds him, "Everything I have is yours. But," the father adds, "when this, your brother, comes home, I cannot help but rejoice. For he was lost, and he's found; he was dead, and he's alive."

How does this parable end? Did the elder brother come in? Did he say, "I see your point, Dad. Maybe my brother left because I'd been such a hard fellow to get along with. Maybe we ought to give him another chance. I'm glad you treated him like you did. I'm going to go in. I'll join in the dancing, in the music, in the barbecue. I'm glad he came home." Or did the older boy stay outside?

Jesus asks his listeners to write the conclusion. For this "older boy" was standing right in front of him as he was telling parables. The religious establishment, the ministers, the church members, and Sunday school teachers who had brought up the issue of the outcasts in the first place—they themselves were the real prodigals.

These three stories dramatically teach us that God is intensely concerned for the "lost." God is like the shepherd who seeks and finds the one lost sheep, and then calls friends and neighbors together to rejoice. God is like the woman who persists until she finds the lost coin, and then calls friends and neighbors together to rejoice. God is like the father who eagerly awaits his lost son and calls his household together to celebrate his return.

We are shortsighted if, without warrant, we conclude that (1) after all, everyone is lost, and hence that (2) membership in God's family is automatic.

In an ultimate sense, everyone is lost, and those

who think they are secure in the kingdom are perhaps most lost of all. But this obscures a critical judgment that Jesus makes. Jesus is not talking about the lost in an ultimate sense. He is talking about a God who discriminates between those who are clearly branded by society as lost, and those whom society considers healthy and not in need of a physician.[6]

Some people are "well" and "found" in an everyday existential sense. The parables of the sheep and coin imply that they may exist in our civilization in numbers that far exceed the presence of the "sick" and "lost." God is not pictured here simply as a God of love, but as a God of *discriminating* concern.

We must take this idea seriously and not try to neutralize it by searching for other passages that appear to repudiate it. We must not systematize this truth out of existence. There are ninety-nine sheep that God does not rejoice over, nine coins that she takes for granted,[7] and one son who (humanly speaking) is somewhat justifiably offended at being overlooked. The elder brother speaks on behalf of a majority of the sheep and coins when he protests against the father's unfairness. Perhaps he also speaks for us.

In his hometown of Nazareth, Jesus delivered an inaugural sermon that gained him applause at first— until the people understood what he was saying! Then they tried to throw him over the nearest cliff.[8]

Jesus began by quoting the familiar prophecy about God's mission being aimed at the poor people, the oppressed, the blind, and the downtrodden. Everybody said, "Amen!"

Then Jesus made the "mistake" of turning the message around, so as to put it into sharper focus. He couldn't have put his foot more firmly in his mouth if he had gotten up to address a middle-class congregation and said, "God doesn't care about this church."[9]

The punch of these "lost" parables comes when we turn them around. They are Trojan-horse parables. Jesus wasn't about to take the same approach that he took before the hometown folks. But he wanted to make the same point to these "white church people" and "Sunday school teachers" who came asking why he spent so much time with outcasts.

Jesus wanted to show them that they were the real outcasts—the prodigals who stayed home. So he lit a stick of dynamite, covered it over with an interesting story, and presented it to them. By the time the "good" people got these parables unwrapped, Jesus and his disciples were a few miles down the road. Perhaps they were still able to hear the explosion. No wonder the "bishops and theologians and key leaders" tried to do away with him.[10]

5
God Against the Rich!

One of our most sacred beliefs is that God is the God of the church, first of all. But thus far the parables have made us wonder whether a vast number of church members may be so swollen with religious pride as to be excluded by the narrow door of the kingdom.

What about the rich? The salvation of the rich is assumed almost as easily as the salvation of the church. The Old Testament has conditioned our understanding to the extent that Proverbs 10:22 is taken by some, at least implicitly, to be the essence of the biblical position: "The blessing of the Lord makes rich" (NRSV).

The parables give us a different view of the wealthy and of what their lives represent. The parables provide the first insight: people don't possess wealth so much as wealth possesses people. Clarence offers this translation and commentary for Luke 12:13-21.

One day when a big crowd of people was following Jesus, someone shouted, "Hey, mister, how about making my brother divide up the inheritance with me?" Jesus turned to him and said, "Say, fellow, has anyone appointed me to be umpire over your financial squabbles?" Then he said to the crowd, "You all really stay on your guard and watch out for all kinds of greediness, because just being rich can't make a man out of you."

Then Jesus told them a story that today may have gone something like this:

The fields of a certain rich man produced abundantly. We don't know the name of this man, so we'll just call him Sam—some of us might even want to call him "Uncle."

Uncle Sam's fields produced an abundance of corn, cotton, peanuts, and soybeans. He had been working on these fields for a long time. He bought them when he and his wife were young. They had worked hard.

Many a time, they had gone out at the crack of day to do the chores. They spent long days plowing, hoeing cotton, trying to make a big crop so they could pay off the mortgage, buy furniture, get a new car, and put the kids through school. Sometimes they even found time to go to church on Sunday.

Occasionally at the close of the day, he and his wife would walk out on the hill back of the house and watch the sun paint its beautiful farewell to the day. They would stand there silently and watch it, and sometimes she would hold his hand and say, "It's pretty, ain't it?" And he would say, "It's pretty, Honey, sure is. It's real pretty."

With his kids, he even found time to hunt arrowheads and to stalk the elusive whippoorwill. There were times when he would gather them on his lap and read to them from *Winnie the Pooh*.

As time went on, these family breaks became rarer. The county agent was there to talk with him about liming his land, contouring, strip farming, soil-building legumes, and all that kind of stuff to make his farm more productive. And there was the stream of machinery salesmen besieging him with all kinds of laborsaving and profit-making equipment.

Increasingly, Uncle Sam became more like the machines that dominated his life. He had little feeling anymore, but what did it matter? He was more productive, and better than that, he was making more profit. Long ago little corncribs had given way to row on row of steel grain bins; his barns became bulging warehouses. His problem now was not how to make crops, but where to store them.

True, he heard that people in other lands were starving, but it was their own fault. They were lazy, ignorant, shiftless, and undeserving. They hadn't mucked and grubbed and scraped like he had; they didn't deserve any better. No sir, no indeed, he wouldn't share his hard-earned goods with them folks. Grain, you know, must be kept in steel bins, not in hungry bellies.

Then one day he looked over his auditor's report and income tax returns. He was quite pleased with the way things were going. He told himself, "Sam, you old codger, you have enough to live it up for the rest of your life. Put your land in the soil bank, man; get a government loan on your grain; and then, boy, head for Florida. Sam, you're going to recline, dine, wine, and shine."

Then God said to him, "*You nitwit!* On this very night all these things are possessing your soul. You don't own them; they own you. And all this stuff you have piled up, whose is it, really?" So the poor, rich farmer was struck with the realization that he would continue for the rest of his life in bondage to the things that had enslaved him all along.

"And," Jesus said, "that's the way it is with a man who sets his heart on money and not on God!"[1]

The parable makes the point that this farmer's *riches* are crying out for his soul. The traditional interpretation is that the man is going to die. Fate or God or some unnamed force is demanding his soul, saying that his time is up. But the Greek text does not say, "This night your soul is being demanded of you." It

says, "This night *they* require your soul of you."
"They" refers to the "many good things" that the
farmer thought he owned.

These things are telling the farmer what to do so
that he can't do what is desired by God, to whom the
"soul" rightfully belongs. This parable warns about
becoming a slave of money—something our credit-
card civilization needs to hear. What we supposedly
possess, often on credit, dictates what we must do to
secure and maintain it.

Jesus introduces another parable that tells us what
wealth demands when it cries out for our souls. The
"soul" is a general term referring to the force that drives
us and motivates and consumes our lives. What is the
effect of this force within us? What are the results when
our riches start giving us orders, as they inevitably do?
Jesus gives us a picture of what happens:

Once there was a rich man, and he put on his tux
and stiff shirt and staged a big affair every day. And
there was laid at his gate a poor guy, a beggar by the
name of Lazarus, full of sores, and so hungry he
wanted to fill up on the rich man's table scraps. On
top of this, the dogs came and licked his sores.

It so happened that the poor fellow died, and the
angels seated him at the table with Abraham. The
rich man died, too, and was buried.

In the hereafter, the rich man, in great agony,
looked up and saw from afar Abraham and Lazarus
sitting beside him at the table. So he shouted to him,
"Mr. Abraham, please take pity on me and send
Lazarus to dip the end of his finger in some water

and rub it over my tongue, because I'm scorching in this heat."

Abraham replied, "Boy, you remember that while you were alive, you got the good things (the good jobs, schools, streets, houses, etc.), while at the same time Lazarus got the leftovers. But now, here *he's* got it made, and you're scorching. And on top of all this, somebody has dug a yawning chasm between us and you, so that people trying to get through from here to you can't make it; neither can they get through from there to us."

The rich man said, "Well, then, Mr. Abraham, will you please send him to my father's house, for I have five brothers; let him thoroughly warn them so they won't come to this hellish condition."

Then Abraham said, "They've got the Bible and the preachers; let your brothers listen to them."

But he said, "No, they won't do that, Mr. Abraham. But if somebody will go to them from the dead, they'll change their ways!"

He replied, "Well, if they won't listen to the Bible and the preachers, they won't be persuaded even if someone does get up from the dead." (Luke 16:19-31)

This is another one of those Trojan-horse episodes in which Jesus conceals his truth. It's a story, not intended to be history. Jesus did not set out to give us a glimpse into the afterlife. It has but one purpose, and that is to portray a truth.

Jesus said, "There was a certain rich man, and he was dressed up in a tuxedo and a white shirt and pitched a big party every day, complete with mint juleps and magnolia blossoms. He had it made! There was also a beggar by the name of Lazarus, sitting at his gate, full of sores. This beggar would have been happy to eat the scraps from the table of the rich man. More than that, the dogs came and licked his sores."

This parable contains a play on words in the original text. In Greek, the word for "beggar" is related to the word for "spit." Lazarus was a "spit-upon one," held in contempt by the rich man.[2]

In Jesus' day one of the most contemptible things you could do to a man was to spit in his face. That still isn't too polite. To oppose such common social contempt, Jesus was playing on this spittle word. This old rich man is dressed up in a tuxedo, holding a conference, inviting all of his wealthy friends, and putting on a big banquet. And poor old Lazarus is lying out there with the sores. And the rich man spit on him.

But what did the dogs do? How did they use their spit? They licked his sores. Spittle was thought not only to show contempt, but also to have healing properties. Jesus healed a man who was born blind by spitting on the ground, making a salve, and touching the man's eyes. Here, spittle was thought to be something beneficial. The rich man was using his spittle to show contempt. How were the dogs using theirs? To heal. In other words, the dogs were acting in a more human way than a human was.

Most people in Jesus' day would catch the symbolism of these dogs. The dogs—the unsaved people, the unchurched people, the Gentiles, the outcasts—they were using their spittle to heal a man. Who was the rich man? He was the person of God's inheritance. He had the law, the prophets, and the writings. He was rich in the sense of his religious heritage. He thought he had an edge on all of God's goodness.

It so happened that the spit-upon man died, and he was carried away by angels to the bosom of Abraham. Jesus had to shift scenery to get over there on the other side of the grave so he could finish his story. Otherwise, his hearers would have been so immediately threatened by truth that they'd have lynched him on the spot. Jesus will bring the parable back to this side of the grave as soon as he gets to a point where it's safe to do so. In the meantime, everyone has relaxed into thinking that Jesus doesn't have any more to say about the here and now.

The beggar was carried away into the bosom of Abraham. This was Jesus' way of saying that history has a habit of reversing itself. The first shall be last, and the last shall be first. The poor beggar was turned upside down. He used to be on the bottom, getting scraps from the table. Now he's sitting at the table with the daddy of the Hebrew race. Lazarus is sitting right next to Abraham. That was a high honor for any Jew, especially one who was full of sores.

Where is the rich man? He is in torment. And he sees Abraham from afar and Lazarus at his bosom. He shouts out, "Oh, Father Abraham, send me my water boy. Water boy! Quick! I'm just about to perish down here. I need a drink of water." That old rich guy had always hollered for his water boy: "Boy, bring me water! Boy, bring me this! Boy, bring me that! Get away, boy! Come here, boy!"

But Abraham throws it right back in his teeth. Abraham says to him, "*Boy!*" Ain't that somethin'? Abraham slings that term back to him for the first time and says, "Boy, you remember that you got the good things while you were alive, and Lazarus got what was left. You got the good schools. Lazarus got what was left. You got the good sections of town and the paved streets. Lazarus got what was left. You got the good churches. Lazarus got what was left.

"You remember that, don't you? Don't you remember that? Back there you were alive, before you died? You got good things. Lazarus got the crumbs that had fallen from your table. Don't you remember that?"

"Hmmm. Seems like I do have a few memories."

"You betcha. Now Lazarus is the guest of honor and you're in great pain. And more than that, there is between us and you a yawning chasm so that those who want to go between can't make it."

This is really the cutting edge of the parable, this yawning chasm. It's broken up traffic. The bridge is blasted. There's a big chasm between 'em. We can't get to you. You can't get to us.

Who dug that ditch? Who dug that chasm? Where did it come from? That rich man knows who dug it. *He dug it!* And why did he dig it? He dug it to break up traffic. He dug it to keep out guys with sores. He didn't want the value of his property to go down when sore people moved into his neighborhood.

You know, you'd better be careful how you dig ditches to keep people out; you might want to cross them yourself some day. Be careful when you blow up bridges. You might want to cross that bridge some day. This rich man is caught in his own trap.

Then he says, "Well, sir, Father, I beg you to send him to my family, for I have five brothers. Let him testify to them, lest they come to the same place of torment that I have come to. I've got five brothers thinking just like I think. They're digging ditches, they're breaking up traffic, they're erecting barriers around themselves. Oh, Father Abraham, I know what a horrible thing this is now. Please let this Lazarus go back and tell my brothers what an awful thing it is to dig chasms."

And ol' Father Abraham says, "They got Moses and the prophets. Let them listen to them." In other words, he's saying, "They got the Bible and the preachers. What's the matter with those guys? Can't they read? Can't they hear? They got preachers all over everywhere who have skill in the interpretation of the Scriptures. Let them listen to what the Scriptures are saying."

"Oh, Father Abraham, they don't listen to those preachers. I know. I sat under preachers for thirty years and never paid attention to a single thing they said. But you just let Lazarus go down there—let him just ooze through the room a few times. I think you'll get some results. But they ain't goin' to listen to the preachers. And they ain't goin' to listen to the Bible."

Abraham said, "Oh, no, if they won't listen to the Bible and the preachers, they won't be persuaded if someone goes to them from the dead. If you can't get results by appealing to their minds and hearts, you're not going to get results by scaring them into the kingdom. You can't populate heaven with refugees from hell."

So this parable is a beautiful dramatization of the fact that the last shall be first, and the first shall be last. And any time you break up traffic, you're blowing the bridges that someday you might want to travel.

We are all accustomed to living with gulfs that keep us from each other: the gulf of wealth, the gulf of pride, the gulf of race, the gulf of sexual identification or orientation. Perhaps we would not admit that we dug these ditches to keep certain people out. We just worked hard and got wealthy; it's not our fault if poor people can't afford to live in our neighborhood, belong to our clubs, or join our church.

The point of this parable that really condemns us is not that we dug the ditch. To a certain extent, if you were born white, if you were born American, and if your family could afford to "civilize" and educate you, then maybe fate did have a hand in digging the ditch. This is the question: What are you and I doing, while we still have time, to fill in that ditch and to overcome the boundaries that shut other people in or out of our fellowship?

Building bridges must become our priority. We can no longer get by with the claim that we are open to anyone who *comes to us. We've got to go to them.* We can't salve our consciences by inviting and "helping" people to become rich along with us. We've got to become poor along with them. The burden of action— bridge-building—is upon us. We must find ways to dispossess ourselves of whatever separates us from the least of our international brothers and sisters.

We must cross over into their world out of compassion for the beggars who sit at our gates. Our own dispossession will go part of the way toward healing the sores of humanity. But, more important, we must dispossess ourselves for our own sakes. This is the punch that the parables deliver most decisively.

We are the victims of the barriers we have erected with the help of fate, circumstance, and the "natural thing to do." We have shut ourselves out of the family of the Father because we have failed to realize that "those who are on the top will be on the bottom." We have failed to realize that, at this very moment, our goods are demanding our souls and receiving them. That is why God cannot be God of the rich.

The United States has 6 percent of the world's population and 60 percent of the world's wealth. To say that God can't be the God of the rich is, therefore, the same as saying that God can't be God of middle-class America.

Our wealth or poverty is not measured by the amount of money we owe on cars, appliances, and homes compared to the amount of money we have in the bank. Practically all of us could plead poverty if that were the standard. It is measured, instead, by the outward comfort of our lives compared to the misery of the masses who are ill-fed, ill-clothed, and ill-housed. By this standard, all of us must admit to being wealthy. *The gulf between ourselves and the poor is the gulf between ourselves and God.*

6
Disturbing the Peace

Two sure signs of culture are amiability and restraint. These virtues carry us a long way into the good graces of civilized society. In our better homes and schools and churches, we have been taught diplomacy, courtesy, and serenity. If cleanliness is indeed next to godliness, composure cannot be far removed.

Imagine our surprise, then, when we discover that smooth, cool civility is sufficient to *disqualify* us from participation in the God Movement. God is not the spiritual Father of us all. He is the Father of the distraught and the impetuous, who reach out in desperation for an answer to injustice.

Most of us would not admit to leading "lives of quiet desperation" (Thoreau). Can the parables sober us and help us recover the foolhardiness that must characterize our citizenship in the kingdom? Is there any recklessness that we can muster, or have we become too civilized for membership in God's family? Have we made ourselves at home with the "peace" of this world? Have we placed too much geographical and emotional distance between ourselves and the world's starving, lonely masses?

The biblical imagery of hungering and thirsting after justice conveys an intensity we often lack. Hungering and thirsting call forth the necessity for daring action. To avoid the need for such action, God planned the ideal Israelite society so that both neighbors and government officials would be unfailing in

71

supplying justice. At their best, the Israelites represented a normative personal and institutional response to the nature of God and to the plight of the oppressed.

> Yahweh your God is God of gods and Lord of lords, the great God, triumphant and terrible, never partial, never to be bribed. It is he who sees justice done for the orphan and the widow, who loves the stranger and gives him food and clothing. (Deut. 10:17-18, JB)

Orphans, widows, and strangers are the oppressed, those for whom God especially cares.[1] If any civilization disenfranchises these people, if any world order overlooks the legitimate needs of its third-world brothers and sisters—those who are strangers to food and clothing—then that civilization forfeits its own right to exist.[2]

God has been merciful to us, who once were strangers to him. Therefore, the imperative for us is transformed from a mandate for mercy to a mandate for simple justice. As a matter of fairness, we are to reflect the goodness that has been shown to us.

We have received such an undeserved abundance that whatever we might give to others, even if we were to deliver our bodies as living sacrifices, would only amount to what is reasonable and right. The following passage demonstrates this new, radical, and liberating perspective that we are to have on life.

Then Rock[3] sidled up and asked, "Sir, how often should I forgive my brother when he keeps doing me wrong? Seven times?"

"I wouldn't say seven times," Jesus replied, "but *seventy times seven!* That's why the God Movement is like a big businessman who wanted to settle the accounts of his customers. As he started to do so, one customer came in who owed a bill of more than ten thousand dollars. He had nothing to pay on the account, so the businessman told the sheriff to put up for sale everything the guy had and apply it to the debt.

"But the fellow did a song and dance. 'Please give me more time, and I'll pay every cent!' he begged. The businessman was touched by the guy's pitiful pleas. So he let him go and marked off the debt. Then that same guy went out and found a little man who owed him a hundred dollars. Grabbing him around the neck, he choked him and said, 'Pay me that money you owe.'

"'Please give me a little more time,' the man begged, 'and I'll pay every cent.' But he refused and, instead, he swore out a warrant for the little man. When the little man's friends found out about it, they were really upset, so they went and told the big businessman all that had happened.

"Then the big businessman sent for the guy who had owed him the huge debt and said to him, 'You lowdown bum! I marked off all that debt for you because you begged me to. Shouldn't you, then, have been kind to that little man just as I was kind to you?'

"Still hot under the collar, he turned the fellow over to the law to be thrown into the clink until every last dime of the debt had been paid. And my spiritual Father will treat you along the same lines unless every single one of you forgives your brother from your heart." (Matt. 18:21-35)

For those of us who have received God's forgiveness, there is no longer any possibility that we can withhold forgiveness from others. Forgiving others is now a matter of justice, of fairness, of loving others as we ourselves have been loved.

Likewise, meeting the needs of others in regard to the necessities of life is no longer a matter of mercy, though the needy may be begging us for "mercy" from their perspective. But from our perspective, we stand in the place of blessing and enjoy the forgiven-seventy-times-seven relationship to God. Hence, it would be hypocritical for us to take Rock's suggestion seriously and stop at seven acts of forgiving in our relationship with those who beg from us. We must be mature as our heavenly Father is mature.

Rock thought that forgiving seven times would be mercy enough. Jesus countered that seven times is not only a shortage of mercy; it isn't even sufficient to fulfill the minimum daily requirements of justice!

Jesus draws us two pictures of society that are not complimentary. Justice has fallen upon hard days. The sources of justice have grown callous; in these two instances, the typical sources are a neighbor (Luke 11) and a judge (Luke 18).

When we look at the first picture, the parable of the

neighbor at midnight, we should remember that the provision of bread for the stranger was a matter of justice within the Hebrew culture. It was not optional. It was not "merciful."

> If a stranger lives with you in your land, . . . you must count him as one of your own countrymen and love him as yourself. (Lev. 19:33-34, JB)

So the following is a parable of the struggle for justice.

> Suppose you have a friend who comes to you in the middle of the night and says, "Hey, neighbor, how about lending me three loaves of bread? A friend of mine has just arrived at my house, and I don't have anything to serve him."
>
> Then you'll call out from inside the house, "Please don't disturb me! I've already locked the door and have got all the kids to sleep. I can't get up and let you have anything."
>
> I really believe that even though you won't get up and let him have something out of friendship for him, you will crawl out and let him have whatever he needs if he keeps yelling and pounding on the door.
>
> So that's why I'm telling you, start asking and it will be given to you; start looking, and you will find; start knocking, and it will be opened to you. For every asker receives, every seeker finds, and to every one who knocks, the door is opened. (Luke 11:5-10) [4]

Jesus is saying that we are in a sad state of affairs if it takes "yelling and pounding" to bring justice. The Greek word for "yelling and pounding" refers to the man's impudence. This man, making such a racket in the middle of the night, is shamelessly disturbing the peace. The demand for justice overrides the demand for civility, for proper procedures, for "wait until morning."

The time for justice is now, so we should be quick to "start asking," "start looking," and "start knocking." The Greek verbs indicate a continuous action, as is consistent with the parable. We are to "start asking" and keep on asking. We are to yell and pound until the door is opened.

To the extent that we possess the world's goods, we should see ourselves as the sleepy and reluctant neighbor in the parable. We should be ashamed that it takes so much clamor to get us to respond to basic human need.

Does the third world have to break down the door of the church to get it to react? Does James Foreman have to disrupt a worship service, no less, and issue a "Black Manifesto"? Whether he does or does not is up to us. How soundly asleep are we? How much rationalizing and red tape do we string out to protect ourselves and perpetuate injustice?

But suppose God is the one who is asleep at midnight. As pointed out in Deuteronomy (10:17-18), God is the one who ultimately "sees justice done, . . . who loves the stranger and gives food and clothing." In the verses that follow this parable in Luke, Jesus implies that the ultimate appeal for justice is to God himself, who gives to those who ask (11:9-13).

We know how to give good gifts to our children, even though we are sinful and our children have to be a little persistent sometimes to get our attention. How much more readily will *God* respond to even our most casual request? He is certainly not asleep nor is he callous to the pursuit of justice. Jesus infers that if it were up to God alone, justice would be done swiftly. By the time the needy one was ready to knock, God would be waiting at the door with the necessary food.

The catch is that *in this world, at this time, it is not up to God alone.* If it were, this parable would be meaningless. God has chosen to act through God's people. This is not primarily a parable about who God is; it is about who we must be. We must be light sleepers. We must not wait for violence to be done before we do justice for the needy at our gate.

Suppose our traveling friend comes to us, and we act on behalf of God as we should. We take him in, even though he is an unexpected guest. But we discover that we don't have anything to serve him. The requirements of justice are beyond our immediate control. We, along with our third-world friends, all become strangers to bread. What shall we strangers do?

In an ultimate sense, we go to God. But in this case, if our appeals to our Christian brothers and sisters have been exhausted, we go to God's appointed representative, the state.[5] In many situations, the state is to be the immediate and perhaps the only possible source of human justice. Now we must resort to these resources of government.

We must not only be light sleepers when the friend

comes to our house, but we must be loud knockers when we appeal to our neighbors on our friend's behalf. The cupboards of the church are bare. The church itself is needy. The church doesn't ask the state for resources it already possesses. We don't take our friend next door if we ourselves can feed him. We don't expect the institutions of government to respond with a compassion that we ourselves don't possess.

Our friends have come to us; we are awake and active on their behalf; but we are powerless. Surely we will not stop knocking just because the people inside the church cannot or will not open the door.

We will go to where the power is. This parable indicates that even though we ourselves are oppressed, we still have the responsibility to go next door and appeal to the institutions of government to fulfill the purpose for which they were appointed.

The state now plays the role of the sleepy and reluctant neighbor. Shall we be timid lest we arouse this threatening giant and incur its wrath? Or shall we create such a nonviolent ruckus that the state will give in to our demands just to be rid of us?[6] If Jesus has indeed come to cast fire upon the earth, it will not be kindled by modest and polite women and men. The God Movement is not made up of such stuff.

God is anxious for us to cultivate this bright aspect of discipleship that our society has taught us to suppress. We live in a cruel world. We cannot be meek and mild on behalf of our friends. There comes a time when we must rise up with all the conviction that is in us and shatter the rationalized, pragmatic procedures that typify our society.

We want bread for our friends. We will not wait until morning. We will not cool our compassion or our tempers. We will not listen to "reason." We will not go through "proper" channels. And we will disrupt and disturb the slumber and the apathy of our culture until justice is served.

This impudence is part of the bright side of discipleship because it is part of the nature of God.

> Yahweh advances like a hero,
> his fury is stirred like a warrior's.
> He gives the war shout, raises the hue and cry,
> marches valiantly against his foes.
>
> "From the beginning I have been silent,
> I have kept quiet, held myself in check.
> I groan like a woman in labor,
> I suffocate, I stifle.
>
> "I will turn mountain and hill to desert,
> wither all their greenery,
> turn rivers to pools
> and dry up lakes.
>
> "But I will make the blind walk along the road
> and lead them along paths.
> I will turn darkness into light before them
> and rocky places into level tracks.
>
> "These things I will do,
> and not leave them undone." (Isa. 42:13-16, JB)

This Old Testament passage is written in the context of a chapter about the servant of Yahweh, who brings true justice (Isa. 42:1-4). One can almost see the Messiah yelling and pounding at the bar of justice and overturning the tables of the money changers at the temple. If our enlightened society calls this behavior "ugly," we must remember that God has a different notion of beauty. Perhaps the measured wisdom of our culture is itself ugly and oppressive.

A companion parable that develops this same idea of the relationship of the Christian and the state is found in Luke 18. In this second drama, there is no doubt that the government, not God or the church, needs to be aroused from its bed of judicial apathy. Jesus is careful to point out that the judge in this story admits to having not even a basic regard for God. Therefore, he cannot represent the church.

> One time in a certain city, there was a judge who didn't believe in God and didn't give a hoot about people. In the same city was a widow, and she came to him repeatedly and said, "Please hear my case against so-and-so."
>
> He put her off for a long time, but finally he said to himself, "Even though I don't believe in God and don't give a hoot for people, yet because this woman has got it in for me, I'll hear her case before she finally nags me to death." (Luke 18:2-5)

The word translated "nags" is a graphic word in the Greek with a violent physical connotation. The verb form literally means "to beat black and blue." Perhaps this widow brought her cane to the courthouse! In any case, we have an intensification of the impudence we discovered in Luke 11.

There are times when causing trouble is the witness we must raise for the sake of justice. There are times when the depth of our concern for something will lead us to overstep the bounds of a common law and order for the sake of a higher law and order.

I do not believe that Jesus wants us *literally* to bruise the body politic. Yet Jesus uses strong language to make his point: what is just in God's eyes is more important than standard operating procedure in the eyes of our culture. If we are to reflect the intensity of God's compassion for the victims of oppression, we must rise above the usual habits of "good citizenship."

Justice and mercy are often seen in Scripture as the fruit of Christian commitment. God requires these instead of rituals and churchmanship. Any culture that has received the light of the gospel is under a tremendous obligation to order its national life according to God's law. Israel failed at the time of Jesus. The United States, which presumes to say that it is "one nation under God," has also failed.

Indeed, the entire Western world is mocked by its steeples and creeds. We have received God's grace, but we have not returned the fruit of obedience. This is why God is prepared to withdraw his grace from the enlightened and "religious" and give it to outsiders, the third world, the "pagans."

A parable in Matthew 21 records this story of God's action. Jesus is speaking to religious leaders who questioned his authority.

"Once there was a farmer who set out a peach orchard, built a fence around it, bought equipment, and put up a packing shed. Then he rented it to some sharecroppers and left. When peach-picking time came, he sent his workers to the croppers to get his share of the fruit. But the croppers took his workers and beat one of them, killed another, and stoned the other.

"So he tried again, this time sending more important workers than before, but the croppers treated them the same way. Finally he sent his son, thinking that surely they would respect *him*. But when the croppers saw the son, they got together and said, 'Hey, there's the old man's boy. Let's kill this cat and take over his estate!' So they grabbed him, and dragged him out of the orchard, and murdered him. Now, when the owner of orchard comes, what will he do to those croppers?"

They answered, "Why, he'll tear those bastards to bits, and let out the orchard to croppers who'll give him his share of the fruit at harvesttime."

Jesus asked them, "Haven't you ever read in the Bible: 'The stone that the craftsmen rejected was selected as the cornerstone. This was done by the owner, and it is an amazing sight for us'?

"Now that's why I'm telling you that the God Movement will be taken out of your hands and turned over to people who will be productive."

The ministers and church people listened to his comparisons and were aware that they were aimed at them. They were dying to arrest him but feared the crowd, who regarded him as a man of God. (Matt. 21:33-46)

The landowner in this parable had fixed up a plot of land. He leased it out to some sharecroppers and went away to spend the winter in Florida. He was going to retire because he was tired of fooling with the farming himself. He was going to come back from time to time to get his share of the fruit.

The parable is directed to the nation Israel. Jesus said to Israel, "God leased you this land. He entered into a contract or covenant with you in good faith, expecting you to carry out your end of the bargain. He sent his servants to you. These were the prophets. And what did you do with them?"

"Well, we took up an offering and gave them an honorarium."

No, that's not what they did with them. Back in those days, a prophet didn't have any better sense than to preach a sermon that the people could understand. And they got the point. Then the prophet got the point, too, along with a few rocks.

"Well," God said, "I'll send them more prophets and try again." So he sent them Isaiah, Amos, Micah, Obadiah, and Malachi. But they took them out and beat them, too. "Oh," God thought, "what kind of folks did I rent my orchard to? What am I going to do? Oh, I know. I'm going to ask my Boy to go up there. He will carry my authority with him, and surely when they see him, they will have respect for him. I'm gonna send him."

God so loved the world that he gave his only Son. He came to his own, and his own received him not. They took him out of the orchard, out on the little hillside, and there they lynched him.

"What do you think is going to happen to those farmers?" Jesus asked. The church people and ministers who had been listening said, "We know what'll happen to 'em. The land will be taken away and be given to somebody who'll act right."

Now, this isn't the judgment of God's severity being handed down on people. It is the judgment of history itself upon nations that do not bring forth the fruit.

This was one of Jesus' parables where the religious people of his day got the point immediately, despite the Trojan-horse technique. Hopefully, we can also get the point that Jesus is making about us proper Christian citizens. God has leased out his orchard to us, and we have at best returned a diluted "faith." We have substituted "worship" for obedience and practicality for reckless faithfulness.

Reasonable people, acting judiciously, crucified Jesus; our civil religion ratifies the verdict. We are the children of propriety. That is why God is in the market for some new farming partners. The broad, heavily traveled path of civilized behavior is not an adequate response to God nor a true reflection of the nature of God.

When I was a teenager in Pittsburgh with access to the family car, my father would often help me by giving directions to various destinations. Dad was a traveling salesman who knew his way around the city. But even for him, Pittsburgh presented problems with its hills, rivers, tunnels, and triangles. Out of hundreds of streets, no two seemed to run parallel. After struggling with a road map and his memory for a while, Dad would often shrug his shoulders and comment, "You can't get there from here."

That's just the way it is with the kingdom of God.

We can't get to that kingdom from here if we are going to stand fast with reason and practicality, law and order, as the highest good; if we are enslaved by the traditional road maps that others pass down to us; if we are thoroughgoing children of our culture.

When you're sitting in a crowded auditorium and you smell smoke, you've got to disturb the peace a little as a matter of justice.

7
Children of Arrogance

Whose children are we? We are children of the church, of mammon, and of culture. These parents have cost us—
- our humility: we see ourselves as "good" people,
- our vulnerability: we have dug a ditch around our lives to keep away the needy, and
- our impetuous zeal for the kingdom: we are quite at peace with *this* world, thank you.

We never decided to leave the kingdom. We never consciously became God's enemies. This is what troubles us. We don't hate Jesus! So why are we cast in the role of outside adversaries? We look, feel, and sound like Christians. Yet the parables have made us out to be villains.

There is a parable that helps us understand our origins and the anatomy of our silent rebellion.

Then he laid before them another comparison: "The God Movement is like a man who planted certified seed in his field. Then after everybody had gone to bed, his enemy came and overplanted the wheat with zizania [wild rice]. When it all came up and started to grow, the zizania was clearly present.

"The farmer's fieldhands came to him and said, 'Sir, didn't you plant certified seed in your field? Then how come it's got zizania in it?' He replied 'An enemy did that!'

"The fieldhands asked, 'Do you want us to go

and chop it out?' The farmer said, 'No, because you might dig up the wheat with the zizania. Let them both grow until harvesttime. Then I'll say to the harvest workers, "Gather all the zizania first and pile it up for burning, and then harvest the wheat and put it in my barn."'"

Then he left the crowds and went into the house. His students gathered around him and said, "Please unravel for us the comparison of the field of zizania."

He answered, "The farmer who planted the certified seed is the Son of Man; the field is the world; the certified seed are the people who do God's will; the zizania are the people who do the will of the evil one; the enemy is the Confuser; the harvest is the fruition of the era; and the harvesters are God's messengers.

"So, just as the zizania was piled and burned, that's the way it will be at the fruition of the era. The Son of Man will send out his messengers, and they'll collect everything in his Movement that's offensive and all the criminals, and they'll burn them in a roaring furnace. In there, they'll be howling and snapping their teeth. Then the just will shine like the sun in their Father's Movement. Now let *that* percolate through. (Matt. 13:24-30, 36-43)

The man in this parable is a real good farmer. He didn't just go out and buy any kind of seed. He got what had been certified by the State Association as purebred. So he planted certified seed in his field. While people slept, his enemy came and planted zizania in the midst of the wheat and went away. This is called overplanting. You plant your field and then somebody comes along and overseeds it with zizania.

Now zizania was that particular obnoxious weed that you paid not to have in there. It's a kind of weed that closely resembles wheat and is difficult to tell from the real thing. The farmer wisely decides to let the wheat and the zizania grow up together until the time of the harvest, when the wheat will be gathered into the barn and the zizania will be put into bundles to burn.

Now, this was a hard parable for Jesus' disciples to crack open. So they came and said to him, "Will you please bust open that story about the zizania? We just can't get it cracked. Rock hammered at it, busted his hammer handle, and didn't get anywhere. Andy tried it. He busted his finger. Nathaniel tried it, and he busted out with some Hebraic expletives." They were havin' one ol' time tryin' to bust open that parable.

What is this story all about? The common interpretation is that Jesus is talking about the end of the world. When the nations get through arguing and bumping each other's heads, there will be one big boom, and that will be the end of things. We'll just have fragments left. The angels will come down here and try to salvage what they can.

But this isn't what Jesus is talking about. He isn't talking about the end of the world as we usually think of it. This termination of the age means the end of the old worldly age. The new age is the age of the family of the Father; it's the revolution. As the revolution comes in, the old age is terminated. Thus the end of the world is taking place all the time.

Where the truth is preached and practiced, there is the end of darkness. Wherever freedom comes in, that is the end of the world for slavery. Wherever anyone preaches the kingdom of God, of the Spirit, there is the end of the world. It doesn't mean the destruction of the world; it means the end of its influence.

For instance, I'm quite sure that one of the reasons Koinonia has run into so much difficulty is because we are surrounded by a lot of people who believe that the plantation system has to be maintained in order to preserve a healthy economic life. They see in the preaching of the gospel of Jesus, and the practicing of it, the end of the plantation system with its exploitation of labor. For them, the preaching of the gospel is the end of the world, the end of their world.

Jesus is saying to these religious people who thought that God was going to go on tolerating the wickedness that was in Israel, "Look here, God planted you a long time ago. He sent you preachers and prophets, and they have preached to you, but somehow or other, they have let the wicked one of the world come in and introduce into your midst all kinds of wickedness. God is not going to tolerate that indefinitely in his kingdom."

We became enemies of God without knowing it. We were planted in secret and grew up as well-disguised intruders. We fooled our neighbors and even ourselves with our pseudospirituality. But the Son of Man knows the unmistakable signs of illegitimacy. We are zizania—imposter children—and God cannot tolerate us in the kingdom. The church, mammon, and culture have operated as sophisticated fronts for the enemy.

If we could give this enemy a name, an appropriate one would be *Arrogance.* In mythology, arrogance prompted a leading angel to claim the place of God; that led to his subsequent dismissal from the heavenly realm.[1] In the Old Testament, arrogance characterized the serpent's approach to Eve: "Did God really say . . . ?" The serpent also planted arrogance within the human family by tempting them to "be like gods."[2]

We think we are far removed from these incidents. We are naive enough to think that we are immune. In truth, we are the victims of a raging epidemic of pride. It has crept into our sacred institutions and made them its breeding ground.

Wealth, religion, and a casual lifestyle are not the origin of our illegitimacy; they are the outward signs. They are the milieu in which pride manifests and reproduces itself. Jesus gets to the root of the problem in his parables against arrogance.

> He gave this comparison to certain ones who had a high regard for their own goodness, but looked down their noses at others: "Two men went into the chapel to pray. The one was a church member, the other an unsaved man. The church member stood up and prayed to himself like this: 'O God, I thank you that I'm not like other people—greedy, mean, promiscuous—or even like this unsaved man. I go to church *twice* on Sunday, and *I* am a faithful *tither* of all my income.'
>
> "But the unsaved man, standing way off, wouldn't even lift up his eyes, but knelt down and cried, 'O God, have mercy on a sinner like me.' I'm telling you, this man went home cleaned up rather than that one. For everyone who puts *himself* on a pedestal will be laid low, and everyone who lays himself low will be put on a pedestal." (Luke 18:9-14)

Two men went up into the temple to pray. One was a Pharisee, and he was a nice Pharisee.[3] He would've qualified as chairman of the board of deacons in any of our churches. He prayed. He was there for midweek prayer meetings every time, which is certainly something. He was a tither, and that's not to be sneered at. And he was a "faster."

That meant he really observed all the religious observances. He was there for Easter; he was there for every holiday and every holy day. He was there for the pastor's anniversary; he contributed quite a bit to the fund for the purchase of the new automobile. He was an active member of the religious establishment.

He was so proud of his record that he was afraid God had lost it. So he reopens the file so that if God, perchance, had lost the original, he could furnish him with a carbon copy. He begins to inform God of just what his qualifications are; and they are considerable.

On the other hand, there was this old publican. Publicans were about like fellow travelers. They collaborated with the Roman military occupying forces to collect the taxes from the Jewish people. They were about the most despised and unpopular people. You couldn't have held up a more despicable person than Jesus did. He lets this man, the lowest man on the totem pole, go to the same temple.

The publican, however, didn't ask God to open his file; he had to begin with just a simple prayer: "O God, have mercy on me, the sinner."

Now, Jesus asks, which of them got his prayers answered? They both did; they both got their prayers answered. The old publican asked for forgiveness, and that's what he got. The old Pharisee asked for nothing, and that's what he got. Read it. He asked for nothing whatsoever. His was one of these informative prayers. He just told God what was going on.

Again the thought returns to haunt us: "For everyone who puts himself on a pedestal will be laid low, and everyone who lays himself low will be put on a pedestal." It is repeated in the parable of the places of honor in Luke 14.

Noting the scramble for the places of honor at the table, Jesus gave some advice to the church leaders who had invited him. "When you are invited by someone to a banquet, don't go immediately to the head table. It might be that some big shot with a higher title than yours has been invited, too, and the person in charge of seating arrangements will have to say to you, 'Please let this gentleman have your seat.' Then with embarrassment, you'll begin to step down to the lower seat.

"But when you're invited, take the most inconspicuous seat, and if the emcee comes in and says to you, 'Hello, my friend. Come on up here,' then you'll feel honored before all the guests. For anyone who promotes himself will be humiliated, and he who humbles himself will be promoted." (Luke 14:7-11)

This keynote against pride binds many of the parables together. Pride accounts for the rampant nationalism of Jesus' time and of our own time. "We are the children of Abraham." "We're Number One." But God strips us naked when he tells us that he can mass-produce children of Abraham out of stones.[4] Pride led the elder brother to promote himself. It tripped the rich farmer into thinking he could "recline, dine, wine, and shine"!

Jesus got into trouble with his friends and neighbors in Nazareth when he offended their pride. He could have asked them for a million-dollar pledge to underwrite his ministry to the oppressed, and they would have supported him. But the suggestion that God might leave them behind in his quest for the "outsiders" was enough to mobilize an instant lynching party (Luke 4:16-30).

We all forget that once we were outsiders. We were the original pile of rocks that God brought to life. If we resist the thought that God could justly return us to the rubble heap, then we are *zizania!* We are still outsiders, and our arrogance in thinking that we deserve to be insiders prevents us from accepting God's gracious offer of adoption.

8
Children of Grace

The parables treated thus far have given us a fresh understanding of the nature of God and a disconcerting picture of discipleship. We have not seen God in the abstract, but we do see God in those concrete situations where his existence touches our own. The parables do not concentrate on God being holy or eternal. They focus on God as a parent.

God's parenting touches us when we realize our lostness and our poverty. We show ourselves to be his children when we respond with a consuming zeal for the things of God: justice and compassion.

I have cast the preceding chapters to show how Jesus' parables make a strong critique; this negative viewpoint was most applicable to Jesus' earliest listeners. Jesus spoke about the lost in Luke 15, but he did so in response to the comment of the "white church people" and "Sunday school teachers."[1] These people were the ones whom Jesus left behind, the "healthy" who had no need of a physician.[2]

The rub came when the good folk realized that God's seeking and waiting for the lost left them alone, on the periphery of the kingdom. That kind of indignity caused many of them to stalk out of the kingdom altogether.

The parable of the rich farmer and especially the one about the rich man and Lazarus reveal a God who is concerned for the poor. But their main thrust is against the rich.

We read of the friend asking for bread in the middle of the night and the widow asking for a hearing from the disinterested judge. These two parables depict a God who rewards those persistently pursuing justice in the midst of an unjust world. But they also have a sting: God ignores those who seek his righteous kingdom at a leisurely and civilized pace. This casual attitude is rooted in the arrogance of those who feel that their own high standing within society is proof of their own virtue, society's wisdom, and God's approval.

It is not sufficient for us to summarize these parables by saying that God loves sinners, poor people, and seekers. Jesus' punch absolutely devastates us: God doesn't seem to care about the righteous, the rich, and the cultured. The people who are most at home in the church are most out of place in the kingdom of God!

Is there any hope then for those of us who stand outside the kingdom as the parables have defined it? Yes. Human nature is subject to change. We must put great emphasis on the fact discussed in chapter 4: the elder son may yet be reunited with his father and his brother.

In all the Gospels, the last verses in the parable of the waiting father, commonly known as the parable of the prodigal son, provide the best example of Jesus extending an olive branch to the church people of Palestine:

> But his older son was out in the field. When he came in and got almost home, he heard the music and the dancing, and he called one of the little boys

and asked him what in the world was going on. The little boy said, "Why, your brother has come home, and your daddy has butchered the stall-fed steer, because he got him back safe and sound." At this, the older brother blew his top and wouldn't go in.

His father went out and pleaded with him. But he answered his father, 'Look here, all these years I've slaved for you, and never once went contrary to your orders. And yet, at no time have you ever given me so much as a baby goat with which to pitch a party for my friends. But when this son of yours—who has squandered the business on whores—comes home, you butcher for him the stall-fed steer.'

But the father said to him, "My boy, my dear boy, you are with me all the time, and what's mine is yours. But I just can't *help* getting happy and whooping it up, because *this brother of yours* was dead and is alive; he was lost and has been found." (Luke 15:25-32)

The elder brother represents the righteous people of Jesus' day, the people who, with some justification, could claim that they had dutifully served God over the years without complaint and without going contrary to his orders. These people felt betrayed because Jesus was spending time with outcasts, even though the righteous people were excluding themselves from his fellowship. Perhaps many of us have the same attitude as this elder brother.

The father does not rebuke his bitter, sulking son

because the son's response is understandable as the immediate reaction of human nature to the situation. But if this elder son had realized that his sonship was of grace and not the result of twenty-or-so years of devotion, he would have overcome his hurt feelings and joined the party.

The mission of the father is to help him go beyond his initial distress. The father "pleads" with him—the Greek word refers to a tender and compassionate appeal. The father calls him "son," a designation that is not routine, best translated by Clarence's phrase "my boy, my dear boy." When the son hears the words "what's mine is yours," he is receiving a genuine invitation.

When we have considered the parables fully, we realize that God does not bar us from the kingdom any more than the father kept his elder son away from the festivities. Only our arrogance can lock us out.

Jesus is delivering these hard parables to us, not as a last word of utter condemnation, but as a final appeal to us to abandon our elder-brother role, our self-assurance, our apathy, our possessiveness, our casual "obedience." We may yet strike a bargain if we truly recognize that our day in court has arrived and has found us to be the children of arrogance.

Clarence spoke of Jesus' concern for us in this way:

While he preached love and kindness, and while a number of his parables are spoken in great tenderness, Jesus nevertheless comes at us with great warning. This is just as a man would urgently warn a child who was about to step on a rattlesnake. We can see in these parables something of

Jesus' great love coupled with a great sense of urgency. As humanity almost steps on the rattler, Jesus leaps at us with a story to warn us of the danger lurking in the grass.

These parables, while they might be frightening, can be tremendously profitable. If there is a rattlesnake in the grass, even though it makes your hair just stand up on end, the best thing for you is to know where it is. It's the unknown snake that has the power to kill.

Luke 13 presents the parable that speaks most clearly to our dilemma and to our hope.

> A fellow had a peach tree planted in his orchard, and one day he came looking for some fruit on it but didn't find anything. He said to the hired hand, "Listen here, for three years I've come looking for some fruit on that peach tree, and I haven't found a peach. Chop it down. Why let it take up space?"
>
> But the hired hand said, "Sir, let it stay just one more year, and I'll hoe around it and put some manure on it. If it should bear fruit then, okay; if it doesn't, chop it down." (Luke 13:6-9)

The comparison, or parable, is made between the peach tree and the nation Israel—the nation that thought of itself as the people of God. The story is open-ended. Does the overdose of grace make the tree fruitful, or does the hired hand have to chop it down a year later? Jesus leaves it to us to complete the story. The father who waited for the prodigal son now waits for the elder brother.

I hope we have already seen that justice and mercy

are only two different ways of viewing the same process. From the standpoint of God, for us to forgive seventy times seven or lay down our lives is only a matter of reasonable justice. From the standpoint of the oppressed, even a few crumbs from our table would be considered undeserved grace. Another parable makes the point more sharply.

> Suppose one of you has a servant chopping cotton or feeding chickens. When he comes to the house that night, would you say to him, "Come on and let's eat"? No, indeed! You would say to him, "Wash up and get supper for me, and wait on me while I'm eating and drinking, and when I get through, then you can have your supper." Does one *thank* a servant for merely doing what he is told? All right, that's the way it is with you. When you've done what you've been told, you should say, "We're but undeserving servants doing our duty." (Luke 17:7-10)[3]

We're but undeserving servants when we consider what we have received from God: mercy. We're only doing what his grace constrains us to do: justice. That happens when obedience takes us beyond a nine-to-five faithfulness. There is no overtime devotion to God. There is no voluntary service. The love of our neighbors is not a measured, punch-the-clock proposition.

The God Movement is like a farmer who went out early in the morning to hire some field workers.

Having settled on a wage of ten dollars a day, he sent them into the cotton field.

Then about nine o'clock, he went to town and saw others standing around idle. So he said to them, "Y'all go on out to the fields, and I'll pay you what's right." And they went. He did the same thing about noon, and again around three.

Then about an hour before quitting time, he saw some others just hanging around. "Why have y'all been knocking around here all day doing nothing?" he asked. "Because nobody has hired us," they answered. "Okay, then y'all can go out to the cotton fields, too," he said.

At the end of the day, the farmer said to his field boss, "Call the workers and pay them off, starting with those who came last and continuing to the first ones." Well, those who came an hour before quitting time were called up and were each paid ten dollars. Now those who got there first thing in the morning supposed that they would get much more; but when they were paid off, they too got ten dollars.

At that, they raised a squawk against the farmer. "These latecomers didn't put in but one hour, and you've done the same by them as you did by us who stood in the hot sun and the scorching wind."

But the farmer said to one of them, "Listen, buddy, I haven't mistreated you. Didn't you and I settle on ten dollars a day? Now pick up and run along. I'm determined to give this last fellow exactly the same as you. Isn't it okay for me to do as I please with what's mine? Or are you bellyaching simply because I've been generous?" (Matt. 20:1-15)

Our heavenly Parent meets the needs of the children with a grace that is sufficient. God does not expect us to bellyache when kingdom latecomers receive a salvation that is equal to our own.[4] The heavenly Farmer does not expect us to balk at paying out to others, regardless of *their* deserts, the grace that we have received regardless of *our* deserts.

To stand "in the hot sun and scorching wind" is, after all, a privilege for us. Likewise, it was a privilege for the elder brother to slave all those years while the son was out squandering his inheritance. *Our obedience is not, in the ultimate sense, a reflection of our own effort; it is a reflection of God's graciousness to us.*

If we don't see membership in God's family as a privilege, then this writing has missed the mark. We are children of grace, or we are not God's children. We may proceed with the reshaping of our lives only as we escape the jail of our own arrogance, which locks us into our old religion, wealth, and culture.

I used to play Monopoly, the board game that rewards sound business judgment and wise financial management. I always got a kick out of passing "Go" and collecting an automatic $200. Often it was the only money I made during the whole game!

The $200 at "Go" was a gift that came to all players, regardless of skill. We assume that they could make a circuit of the board without landing in jail or drawing that terrible card that read, "Go directly to jail. *Do not* pass Go. *Do not* collect $200." This "Go" money was really a gift, even though we anticipated it because the rules of the game provided for it.

The salary that the workers in the cotton field

received at the end of the day was likewise a gift. *In the first place, just to be invited into the cotton field was a gift.* The complaint of the full-time workers was short-sighted and ill-advised, though it might have been justified in a narrow sense of what is fair. They forgot that they too had benefited from the employer's generosity when they were first given jobs.

Thus we see that God's grace is meant to be comforting; it may also be discomforting. It demands that we receive it as grace, remember it as grace, and grant others equal access. No one has an earned "right" to grace; we are all on the same slippery footing when it comes to our standing before God.

When we resent God's generosity to others, we undermine and refuse the grace that comes to us. So we must judge others as we have been judged; we must forgive as we have been forgiven; we must love as we have been loved. Thus we show ourselves to be children of grace rather than children of arrogance.

In chapter 7, on the parable of the zizania, we saw that God could recognize impostor children even when it was hard for us to sort them out. But there is a way to recognize our inner child of arrogance even when it masquerades as a child of grace.

Arrogance generates a proud thanksgiving: "O God, I thank you that I'm not like other people." Grace generates unabashed love. Arrogance is as "proper" and "dignified" as Simon, the church member described in connection with the parable of the two debtors. But the woman who was so uncivilized as to publicly bathe Jesus' feet with her tears proved by her *zealous* love the sincerity of her gratitude.[5]

A certain church member invited Jesus home for dinner. He accepted and went into the church member's house and sat down. Then a shady lady of the town, who had heard that Jesus was being entertained at the church member's home, bought a bottle of high-priced perfume. She sat at his feet sobbing, and her tears began to wet his feet. She dried them with her long hair and kissed his feet and dabbed on some of the perfume.

When the church member who had invited Jesus saw what was going on, he thought to himself, "If this fellow were a real man of God, he would recognize the kind of woman who's fondling him and know that she's a shady character."

Then Jesus said to him, "Simon, I want to talk with you about something."

He said, "Why sure, Doctor, go right ahead."

"Two men were in debt to a certain banker. One owed five hundred dollars, the other fifty. When neither of them could pay up, the banker wrote off the debt of both. Which of the two would you think was the more grateful?"

Simon scratched his head and said, "Why, I suppose it was the one who was relieved of the larger debt."

Jesus said to him, "Right you are!" Then he turned to the lady and said to Simon, "Do you see this lady? When I came into your home, *you* didn't even give me *water* for my feet, but *she* has bathed my feet with her *tears* and dried them with her hair. You didn't even shake *hands* with me, but *she*, ever since she got here, has lovingly kissed my *feet*. So let me point out to you, Simon, that she has been relieved of a heavy load of sin, as evidenced by her great gratitude."

Then he said to her, "Your sins are gone."

And the guests at the table whispered among themselves, "Who does he think he is—forgiving sins!"

He said to the lady, "What you've just done has been the making of you; keep it up—with my blessing." (Luke 7:36-50)

The grace of God is amazing because of the forgiveness that it offers to us: "Your sins are gone." It is amazing because of the discomfort it causes to those who witness its operation. "Who does he think he is—forgiving sins!"

It is amazing because it effectively binds us to a duty that otherwise would constitute overtime devotion: "What you've just done has been the making of you; *keep it up*—with my blessing."

9
Counting the Cost

Now we are working with a ray of hope. We have come to grips with the subtle arrogance within us. Jesus has knocked us off our high horse, but he has acted to save us, not to humiliate us. We have been stripped of our illusions about our religion, our wealth, and our culture; we are at a critical juncture in our journey toward the kingdom. We must do more at this point than try to avoid rattlesnakes.

> When a filthy spirit comes out of a man, he wanders through unwatered areas looking for a home. Finding none, he says, "I'll go back to my house that I left." When he does so, he finds it vacant, cleaned up, and painted. Then he goes and rounds up seven other spirits more wicked than himself, and they all move in and live there. So the man is worse off at the end than he was at the beginning. (Matt. 12:43-45)

There is no virtue in an empty house, even if it is cleaned up and painted. There is no virtue in a negative religion. So we must not be content, even assuming that we have been able to avoid the pitfalls that the parables have pointed out to us.

Jesus called the Pharisees "whitewashed tombs full of dead men's bones" (Matt. 23:27). Sometimes our view of proper religion amounts to little more than a removal of the bones. The parable of the empty house reinforces the idea that a creative passionate zeal is

105

required if we are to gain the kingdom treasure.

The purpose of this chapter is to probe and channel our enthusiasm in the right direction. Remember the seed that sprouted quickly, only to wither in the shallow soil. Our zeal needs to be deep and persevering. We need to be aware of the extended cost involved in following Jesus. No degree of devotion can be too extreme a response to God's grace. Jesus pointed out the need for this kind of realistic reckoning during one of his journeys.

Quite a crowd was trailing him, and he turned and said to them, "If anyone is considering joining me, and does not break his primary attachment for father and mother and wife and children and brothers and sisters and, indeed, for his own life, he simply cannot belong to my fellowship. Anyone who does not accept his own lynching and fall in behind me cannot belong to my fellowship.

"If any of you were intending to put up a building, wouldn't you first sit down and figure out the cost, so you could see if you had enough to finish it? Otherwise, you might lay out the foundation, and because you didn't have funds to go any further, people would begin making cracks about you, saying, 'This fellow is a great hand at starting things, but he can't carry through on them.'

"Or suppose a king were going out to battle against another king; wouldn't he first sit down and determine whether or not, with his ten thousand men, he could face an enemy of twenty thousand? If he figures he can't, then while there is still distance between them, he should send a delegation to seek for terms of peace.

"So that's the way it is with you. Every one of you who doesn't throw in his entire fortune cannot belong to my fellowship." (Luke 14:25-33)

These parables of the incomplete building and the king's warfare point to the necessity for understanding the ultimate cost of discipleship. Jesus wants us to be fully aware of the implications of being children of God's grace. The context of these two parables outlines two of the requirements: "Anyone who does not accept his own lynching" and "who doesn't throw in his entire fortune cannot belong to my fellowship."

Are we serious enough about entering the kingdom that we sever ourselves from family ties, earthly security, and all the dreams we nurture for ourselves? Are we prepared to throw everything up in the air, including our schooling and our careers, our possessions and our ideas? Or are there certain relationships and realities that control us?

God is giving us fair warning that he will touch us at every point to test whether our commitment is total. We can't bluff our way into his family. We will be a laughingstock to both God and ourselves if we permit anything to separate us from the consuming priority of the kingdom. Like the plight of the empty house, our fate then will be worse than if we had never taken Jesus seriously in the first place.

Jesus investigates our readiness by means of three short dramas recorded in Luke 9.

While they were going along the way, somebody said to him, "I'll live your life, regardless of where it takes me."

Jesus replied, "Foxes have dens, and the birds of the sky have nests, but the Son of Man has nowhere to hang his hat."

Then he said to another, "Share my life."

"Okay," he said, "but let me first discharge my family obligations."

Jesus told him, "Let the people of the world care for themselves, but *you*, you spend your time promoting the God Movement."

Still another said, "I will share your life, sir, but let me first work things out with my relatives."

To him, Jesus replied, "No one who commits oneself to a course of action, and then keeps looking for a way out of it, is fit material for the God Movement." (Luke 9:57-62)

When Jesus said, "The Son of Man has nowhere to hang his hat," he was trying to show the totality of the demands of the kingdom. He was not going around looking for people that he could bait by offering a better job:

"You can follow me."

"How much are you paying? I'm getting $100 a week."

"Well, I'll give you $125."

That isn't the way the Lord gathered apostles or disciples. He made it clear to them that it was going to be costly, just as it had cost him, and that they might not have any place they could call home. The person in the second drama, in response to Jesus' request to share life, literally said, "Let me first go and bury my daddy."

Jesus said to him, "Let the dead bury their own dead, but you go and proclaim the new order of the Spirit."

At first sight it might appear that Jesus was being rather rude to this fellow. Here he's saying, "My father died. Can I go to the funeral? I'll come right after the funeral. I'll be right with you."

We misunderstand if we think that's what he means. This man's father wasn't dead; he was still very much alive and kicking around. Why did they want to bury him if he was still alive? Well, in those days, the expression "to bury somebody" meant to live with them until they died, then put them away, and then you were free. It might take you ten years to bury somebody. To bury your father meant to discharge your obligations to your father.

In the first situation, Jesus places the obligation to the kingdom above your material welfare. In the second one, he places it above your relationship to society. Even your father and your relatives can't take priority over the demands of the kingdom of God. If your father can't take precedence, how much less could your friends? So the kingdom is not a matter of what other important people are going to say or think. Your highest loyalty goes to God.

You can't come face-to-face with the kingdom of God and respond, "I like this idea of the God Movement, but you know, I got a spouse and some children. I gotta raise them. Let me get them up out of the way and off to college and through college. Let me pay for my house and all these things. And then, when I get free from all these obligations, I think it'd be nice to retire into the kingdom of God." Jesus said, "The kingdom of God just isn't an old folks' home. You don't retire into it. I want you to get busy *now*."

A third would-be disciple said, "Lord, I will follow you, but first let me go home and draw up a contract with my kinfolks or with my brothers and sisters." Some translations simply record that he wanted to say farewell, but the Greek carries a much more extensive idea than that.

This fellow is really saying, "I want to join this movement, but I don't like this idea of having to give up all I've got. Now, my pappy is quite well off, and he's gonna leave a nice estate when he dies. I wanna go back there and get a lawyer to draw me up an agreement that if I go off with you, I am still in the family inheritance and get my share. I don't wanna take the risk of this God Movement. I wanna protect myself."

In other words, he wanted an escape hatch so that if this movement folded up, he'd have something to go back on. He wanted what we call a "scat-hole." Down South, we cut a little square hole in the bottom of the door so the cat can have some way to come and go. When you say "Scat," he's got some way to go without you gittin' up and openin' the door for him. This boy wanted him a scat-hole so that if the sailin' got rough, and he had to get out of a situation real quick, he could scat.

A lot of folks don't wanna cut loose of everything and jump into this God Movement. They wanna say, "Well, what if this thing folds up?"

We had a lady one time come up and visit us at Koinonia. She was very lonely. I'd say she was in her early forties. She came up in her old jalopy car, and she was rather shabbily dressed. We talked to her for several days. She said, "You know, I like it here. I believe I'd like to just live here."

We said, "That's fine. We'd be glad to have ya."

And she said, "What do I do to join up?"

"Well, just come on and join with us. I presume you don't have much. You can just stay on."

She said, "Oh, well, I have a good bit of property down in New Orleans."

"How much do you have?"

"Oh, I guess I own maybe $90,000 worth."

"Well, the first thing you'll have to do is get rid of that."

She said, "What do you mean? I can't do that!"

"But then you can't come here."

"But I can't give away my possessions. Suppose this thing were to fold up and I had given away everything I owned. Then where would I be?"

I said, "Then you'd be in the same place as the rest of us would be."

"But . . . can't I bring my money and put it in here?"

"No, ma'am, this is the one place you can't put it."

"How come I can't put it in here?"

"Well," I said, "one reason is that you got more money than all the rest of us put together. If you want to put all your money in here, the first thing we'd do would be to sit down under a pecan tree and start discussing theology. But we need to work. We don't need that kind of money. It'll make us lazy, and it'll make mere theologians out of us, and we don't want that to happen to us.

"In the next place," I said, "in your mind, you'll be like a guardian angel to us. You'll expect each of us to tip our hats to you and thank you for what marvelous things you've done for us. We don't tip our hats to anybody, and we don't want you comin' in here with a lot of money.

"In the last place, the reason you can't bring it here's because you look like a very lonely person. Unless I miss my guess, the only friends you've ever had have been those who have wanted to help you spend your money."

She said, "You're right. I don't believe I've ever had a real friend who loved me for what I am. They've always loved my money."

"And if you bring that money here," I said, "you'll always have a sneaking suspicion that the reason we wanted you here was not for what you are, but because of your money. The only way you can get a clear answer to that is to go, sell your possessions, give the money to the poor, and come back here without a dime. Then you'll know whether we love you for what you are or for what you have. You'll get your answer."

She said, "I . . . I just can't do it." And she got in her old jalopy and drove off.

As she did, I turned to my wife and we almost said in unison, "There goes the female rich young ruler." She wanted a scat-hole. She wanted an escape. She wanted to trust her little $90,000 when she needed to learn to trust in God, whose riches are untold.

There is a sense in which this total giving is a prerequisite for entering the kingdom of God. When we enter the kingdom, we sign over to God all of our possessions and all of our energies. But there is also a sense in which our emptying of ourselves is a gradual unfolding of our lives within the kingdom.

Jesus gave up his life when he decided to become Emmanuel, God with us.[1] He carried out that commitment during a thirty-three-year ordeal that culminated at the cross. It is an academic question if we ask when he actually died—whether in Bethlehem, at his baptism, at Golgotha, or gradually throughout his ministry.[2] His death was inevitable.

We need to follow the example of Jesus emptying himself.[3] The implications of total commitment are set in motion. We enter the arena knowing that we will never emerge alive and intact. This entrance, this "death," is the beginning of discipleship. We have begun to respond to our overdose of grace. The ray of hope has become, for us, a rainbow.

10
Trade with These Ideas

The hope for liberation becomes a reality for us when we *act* upon the ideas that the parables have imparted to us.

A man had two boys. He went to the older one and said, "My boy, go work in the orchard today." He said, "Will do, Pop," but he never did. Then he went to the younger one and told him the same thing. But the boy said, "I won't go." Afterward he felt like a heel and did go. Which of the two obeyed his father? (Matt. 21:28-31)

Attitude and motivation are an important part of discipleship, but action is emphasized in this brief story. Jesus was aware of the temptation to "spiritualize" obedience. We feel compassionate; we desire justice. But such emotions are not in themselves sufficient. George MacDonald has said, "Talking and not doing is dry rot." Sincere grappling with ideas is not the same as obedience. Praying for God's blessing on others is not the same as giving a blessing or being a blessing to others.

If we act without verbalizing our intentions, we are closer to the kingdom than if we fail to act despite our noble proclamations and inclinations of the heart. We have to do more than mouth the ideas of the God Movement. We have to trade with these ideas.

It's like a businessman who was leaving town for a long time and called in his assistants and turned over his investments to them. He made one responsible for about five hundred thousand dollars, another two hundred thousand, and another a hundred thousand—according to each one's ability—and then he left town.[1]

Right away the man with the five hundred grand got to work and made five hundred more. The man with the two hundred grand did the same and made another two hundred. But the guy with the hundred G's went and rented a safe-deposit box and put his boss's money in it.

After a long time, the boss returned and called his assistants together for an accounting. The one with the five hundred thousand brought his other five hundred thousand and said, "Sir, you let me have five hundred grand; look, I've made another five hundred." The boss said, "Splendid, you good and responsible worker! You were diligent with the smaller sum; I'll entrust you with a larger one. You'll be a partner in my business."

Then the one with the two hundred G's came and said, "Sir, you let me have two hundred thousand; look, I've made another two hundred." The boss said, "Splendid, you good and responsible worker! You were diligent with the smaller sum; I'll entrust you with a larger one. You'll be a partner in my business."

Well, the hundred-grand man came up and said, "Sir, I know you are a hard-nosed man, squeezing pennies you haven't yet made and expecting a profit before the ink has dried. I was plain scared to take any chances, so I rented a safe-deposit box and put your money in it. Look, you've got every cent."

But his boss replied, "You sorry, ornery bum! You knew that I squeeze pennies I haven't yet made, and expect profits before the ink dries. Then you should have turned my money over to the bank so that upon my return I would get back at least my principal with interest. So then, y'all take the money away from him and give it to the one with the millions.

"For it will be given to everyone who has the stuff, and he'll have plenty; but the man who doesn't have the stuff will have even what he has taken away from him. Now as for this useless critter, throw him in the back alley. That'll give him something to moan and groan about." (Matt. 25:14-30)

Jesus tells this story to his followers while they are on their way to Jerusalem, near the end of his ministry. It was the last week before his death, and Jesus had been talking about the revolution and so forth; all his disciples were excited. They were wondering whether they were going to have a press conference or take over the airport and the telephone exchange. Excitement was in the air. Perhaps the revolution was about to burst out immediately with overwhelming force. To answer that kind of thinking, Jesus told the parable of the talents.

I've heard so many sermons preached on this idea, "Give your talents to the Lord." They got that thing backward. The Lord gives his talents to us. A talent is not some skill. We go around saying, "He's a great athlete. He should consecrate his talent to the Lord. She's a great organist. She should be an organist for the Lord." But this isn't what Jesus is saying.

What are these talents? Are they money? No, Jesus had no money to give. What did he have? What is the stock-in-trade of a great teacher? It's his ideas, his concepts, his teachings, [his saving actions for the kingdom]. He leaves them to his followers.

All these three years, Jesus has been "talenting" the disciples. Now he's saying, "You want me to come in here and pull some angels out of the sky and set up a revolution? Oh, no. Over all these months together, I've been giving you the currency of the kingdom. If it comes, it's gonna come by your doin' business with what I've turned over to you."

To us he says, "I've turned over to you the idea [and reality] of brotherhood and sisterhood."

Some of us can say, "Yes, Lord, I got out and dealt with that idea and multiplied it."

But others of us turn in an accounting like this: "Yes, Lord, I remember you talkin' about brotherhood, but you know, I was scared. I started to preach a sermon on that on race relations Sunday, but Deacon Jones said, 'Hmmm.' You know I didn't want to upset the deacon. No point breakin' up your church.

"Besides, Deacon Jones is one of our major tithers, and he's got something to tithe. So, Lord, I was scared, I was scared of this whole proposition, and I buried this idea of brotherhood."

"I gave you the idea of peacemaking," Jesus says.

"Yes, Lord. But you don't understand the civilization we live in. You gotta talk force. Force is the only language most folk understand today. Really, it's the only language people know how to talk. So, Lord, I had a chance to witness for peace, but I was kind of scared somebody might identify me with these flower children. So I just buried the whole thought."

We've all been given ideas, perhaps not in equal proportion to others. Maybe we haven't done any postgraduate work, but we've got hold of some explosive ideas. We say, "I might lose out tradin' on these. I might lose my neck or my job or my house."

And we're right. This is risk capital Jesus gives to us. But that doesn't excuse us from activity. This little ol' fellow in the parable didn't steal anything from his boss. In fact, he restored everything. He just didn't do what he was told.

Discussing talents isn't a test of talent activity. This assistant had read a book on talent preservation and a book on economics. He was quite knowledgeable on the present value of a talent; he held conferences on inflation and deflation of the talent. He just never got to work. He never put it out there and traded with it.

Now let me tell you, we don't have much more time to do business with the kingdom ideas. It's later than we think. We've caught a glimpse of the gold in God's storehouse. The time of harvest is here. If we don't get off our back ends and start doin' somethin' with these ideas, God Almighty is gonna take these talents that he's turned over to the church and give them to a people that will bring forth the fruits. They might not be a people that we will agree with.

This punch parable is one of Jesus' ways of saying, "You better get up and git! I've given you these ideas, turned over to you my treasure. Now, what are you gonna do with them? Are you gonna wrap them up in some theological junk, or are you gonna get out in the streets and do business with these ideas?"

What are these ideas that are so crucial? Our examination of the parables gives us at least the following new directions for our lives:

1. *The kingdom of God is now.* The parables communicate the urgency of the moment. They focus our attention upon this life—the grace we receive and the obedience we render.

2. *The kingdom of God calls for dramatic action on our part.* We can't just think about God's ideas; we must put them into practice.

3. *The kingdom of God is a gradual process.* We will be consistently disheartened until we are able to accept this reality.

4. *The process involves suffering and powerlessness.* Our continuing goal is to know Christ by sharing his humble beginnings and experiencing his servanthood.

5. *The process is the result of our dependency upon God.* He is our Father and Mother. We are his children. Our lives are a response to and a reflection of the grace of our heavenly Parent.

These ideas transform our lives as we permit them to condition our outlook on life and as we act upon them. We can grasp their future implications by considering the twin parables of the mustard seed and the leaven.

Then he said, "What is the God Movement like, and with what shall I compare it? It's like a mustard seed that a man plants in his garden; it keeps growing until it becomes a big bush, and the birds in the sky make its branches their home."

And again he said, "With what shall I compare

the God Movement? It's like yeast which a house-
wife mixes in three cups of flour until it all rises."
(Luke 13:18-21)

The mustard seed is the smallest of seeds;[2] when it
grows, it becomes a bush, big enough for birds to come and
build their nests in it. The old birds probably flew over that
seed many a time and didn't even think it was worth noticing;
it just wasn't even worth pecking at. They passed it by.

Yet it began to sprout. The seed has life resident in it.
There's a big difference between a seed and a grain of sand.
You plant a grain of sand, and it doesn't matter how much
rainfall and sunshine you have; you're not going to get an
increase. But you plant a seed, and you'll get some action.

Jesus is saying that these kingdom ideas are viable and
real; they're not sterile. Now, if we could just get hold of some
of these ideas in some of our pulpits, it could blow these pulpits and church buildings all to pieces.

The seed is a viable kind of thing that has a habit of push-
ing its way even against great difficulties. Just a few weeks
back, we got through planting peanuts. You put the peanut
seed two or three inches under the ground. We had a big,
hard, packing rain.

I thought, "Oh, my goodness, that little old peanut seed
will never to able to break that hard crust." But a few days
later, we went out there and saw a tiny Spanish peanut seed
lifting a clod of dirt twenty times bigger than it was, just
pushin', sayin', "Get out of the way, clod, I'm movin' to God."
And that little old seed came on out of there.

You can't keep life down. So Jesus says that if you have
kingdom life in you, you move on in spite of the most terrible
difficulties and hindrances. On and on the kingdom goes,

beginning now. The power, he says, is like leaven that just reaches out and goes through the whole lump.

The kingdom of God comes gradually, but it still is an urgent process. The idea of urgency has been implanted within us by several parables already discussed. We especially note the parables of the hidden treasure and the pearl of great price, along with the parable of the man on his way to court.

Nevertheless, we should not embark upon our lives of discipleship thinking that our implementation of mercy and justice will reach immediate fruition. We plant powerful seeds of love. They work silently and persistently to accomplish God's will. There is no fanfare, no world-beating display of strength. But within the humblest act of obedience to God, there is the assurance of victory.

The irony of the parable of the mustard seed is that the birds that might have initially ravaged the man's garden remain to enjoy its benefits. They nest in the branches of its vegetation. Even our enemies will be won over to the kingdom and healed.[3] Not only does the small produce the great, but a narrow hostility is swallowed up by a more comprehensive fellowship.

When you see that even those who "call you names, and harass you and tell all kinds of false tales on you" are your eventual brothers and sisters, then you will not seek revenge, but will be "cheerful and good-humored."[4]

When you ask, you might be a person with impure motivation. When you seek, you might be acting on behalf of only one of the world's needy. When you knock, you might be pounding on the door of only one of the world's many oppressors.[5] Nonetheless, you are initiating a process that will result in justice rolling on like a river and righteousness like an ever-flowing stream.[6]

As it was in the parable of the sower, so it will be in your life: one solitary sustained response to the grace of God will bring forth a hundred, or sixty, or thirty times the initial investment.

So we must trade with the idea that our actions are invincible, even though they may be surrounded by a sea of inhumanity and godlessness for as long as we live. We must trade with the idea that our own lives represent the initial lump that is leavened. Transformation is possible. We can be "raised" now to the new reality of life within the kingdom as we give ourselves to God, who gives us the power to become children of God.[7]

The ultimate victory of our course sustains us, but we should not be concerned with the *strategy* of victory.

This is what the kingdom of God is like. A man throws seed on the land. Night and day, while he sleeps, when he is awake, the seed is sprouting and growing; *how, he does not know.* Of its own accord the land produces first the shoot, then the ear, then the full grain in the ear. (Mark 4:26-28, JB, emphasis added)

We loose the seeds of mercy upon the world. They do their work. We are the bearers and sowers of the kingdom of God, not the architects. God has scattered us in the same way that we are to scatter God's truth.

But we also *are* the seed of the kingdom. The leaven that is placed within the meal is the leaven of our own witness. We are the salt of the earth and the light of the world.[8] And the most devastating idea that God asks us to incarnate is captured in this instruction:

> Jesus then said to his students, "If any want to walk my way, they must abandon themselves, accept their lynching, and share my life. For those who aim to save their life will lose it, and those who lose their life for my cause will find it. (Matt. 16:24-25)[9]

So we do not merely *observe* the gradual process of the kingdom coming; we also *participate* by losing our lives. The impact of this concept leaves our old way of thinking in a shambles. How could there be a sharper contrast between our past life and our present life? How could there be a higher cost? How could there be a greater love?

> I tell you, most solemnly,
> unless a wheat grain falls on the ground and dies,
> it remains only a single grain;
> but if it dies,
> it yields a rich harvest.
> Anyone who loves his life loses it;
> anyone who hates his life in this world
> will keep it for the eternal life. (John 12:24-25, JB)

This is why we can never incorporate and organize and strategize the God Movement. We would be too inclined by our own natures to promote and perpetuate our own existence. We would not allow ourselves to give away our organization, our possessions, and our lives.

Everything has to be lovely. Everything has to work. Everything has to be practical. Everything has to come out right. The story has to end by saying that "they lived happily ever after." We don't want a story that doesn't end that way. So anything that comes in to break up the happy ending—to end the pragmatic way we live—why, we just don't want it. We want to get rid of a God who calls people to die for him, whose own life winds up on a cross. He just isn't the kind of God we want around us.

But Jesus said that the life of his disciples would be life in the shadow of a cross. It's a dying kind of living. He said that you don't know whether it will work or not. Why don't you break off a few chunks of life and try? You experiment with everything else. Break off a few years, a chunk of your life, give it in this bold experiment, and see what happens.

If we are only concerned to provide for our supposed personal righteousness and to maintain the cleanliness and composure of our empty house, then we will not venture out with these ideas. We will be content to bury them beneath our preaching or to adopt them as the playthings of our minds. To trade with the idea of dying, we must welcome the persecution and poverty that come our way as a result of our unconditional servanthood.

Servanthood is the kingdom process whose small beginnings carry us through suffering to resurrection.

All we really want is "to know Christ and the power of his resurrection and to share his sufferings by reproducing the pattern of his death."[10] We bring good news to the poor, and we help the oppressed. In these works of mercy, we become the poor and the oppressed. This is our dying, and it is the finding of our lives.

11
The Works of Mercy

In chapter 6, on "Disturbing the Peace," we considered the close relationship between justice and mercy. God has been merciful to us, and we must reflect that mercy in our relations with others as a matter of fairness. In that chapter we focused on the pursuit of justice. In this chapter we focus on the works of mercy.

The difference in terminology and content is somewhat arbitrary. One can't love tenderly without acting justly. If the works of mercy are carried out, they will be sufficient in themselves to disturb the peace, even though yelling and pounding and persistent nagging may not immediately enter into the picture.

Jesus found himself in trouble because he was serious about doing works of mercy. He traded with the idea that the necessity for compassion overrides the protocol considerations that were of paramount importance to the religious establishment. "Is it proper to eat with sinners?" "Is it proper to heal on the Sabbath?" For Jesus, mercy always took precedence over any human concept of propriety.

This chapter is entitled "The Works of Mercy" because that's what mercy is in the New Testament. It is not simply an inward feeling of pity or compassion; it is a roll-up-your-sleeves endeavor. We have come a long way together through the parables. We have left behind our old lives, and we have embraced new ideas.

Now we are off the drawing board and out of the

classroom. We have counted the cost and have given our lives. At some point during the long night of our prayer and struggle, we have crossed an invisible boundary. We have put our hands to the plow, and we shall never look back. We are God's new farming partners, and we are scattering seeds of mercy that will eventually grow and nourish all of our friends and enemies alike.

Mercy is not an abstract consideration in the teaching of Jesus. *We must be careful, therefore, not to substitute analysis for implementation.* Mercy is not the subject for our doctoral dissertation; it is the outpouring of our sweat and tears. We must not fall into the trap of the adult Bible class teacher who was more concerned with theory than with practice:

> One day a teacher of an adult Bible class got up and tested him with this question: "Doctor, what does one do to be saved?"
>
> Jesus replied, "What does the Bible say? How do you interpret it?"
>
> The teacher answered, "Love the Lord your God with all your heart and with all your soul and with all your physical strength and with all your mind; and love your neighbor as yourself."
>
> "That is correct," answered Jesus. "Make a habit of this and you'll be saved."
>
> But the Sunday school teacher, trying to save face, asked, "But . . . er . . . but . . . just who *is* my neighbor?"
>
> Then Jesus laid into him and said, "A man was going from Atlanta to Albany, and some gangsters

held him up. When they had robbed him of his wallet and brand-new suit, they beat him up and drove off in his car, leaving him unconscious on the shoulder of the highway.

"Now it just so happened that a white preacher was going down that same highway. When he saw the fellow, he stepped on the gas and went scooting by.

"Shortly afterward, a white gospel song leader came down the road. When he saw what had happened, he too stepped on the gas.

"Then a black man traveling that way came upon the fellow, and what he saw moved him to tears. He stopped and bound up the man's wounds as best he could, drew some water from his water jug to wipe away the blood, and then laid him on the back seat.

"He drove on into Albany and took him to the hospital; the black man said to the nurse, 'You all take good care of this white man I found on the highway. Here's the only two dollars I got, but you all keep account of what he owes. If he can't pay it, I'll settle up with you when I make a payday.'

"Now if you had been the man held up by the gangsters, which of these three—the white preacher, the white song leader, or the black man—would you consider to have been your neighbor?"

The teacher of the adult Bible class said, "Why of course, the nig—I mean, er . . . well, er . . . the one who treated me kindly."

Jesus said, "Well, then, *you* get going and start living like that!" (Luke 10:25-37)

Jesus was teaching at a time when racial prejudice was terrific. Jews and Samaritans had no dealings with each other, and Jesus had to be careful with what he said. One day, a fellow stopped him. "By the way, Master, I want to ask you a question. What's the first and great commandment?"

This fellow was a scribe, and a scribe was a combination of Bible teacher and an expert in religious law. So we might call him a lawyer in addition to being a Sunday school teacher.

This young lawyer had just gotten out of law school. He had that question on his final exams, and he wanted to see if Jesus knew it.

Jesus said, "Well, Colonel, how do you read it?" He threw it back at him. And this lawyer started spoutin' it off. He'd learned it in class.

Jesus responded to his recitation by saying, "You've got it right, Colonel. You've got it right. You live that way, and you will have life."

"Oh," the lawyer said, "now, I didn't mean I was gonna live by it. I just love to quote it." You know how some people quote Scripture. They don't mean any harm by it; they love to hear it. They just don't want to live by it.

The lawyer began to pick a little flaw. You know, lawyers can get you by hittn' on technical details. So this lawyer said, "Well, there's one little point there that needs clarifying. Who is my neighbor?"

That young lawyer should have known how the preachers had all agreed that anybody was your neighbor provided he was one of the pure blue-blooded aristocratic faithful. As long as he was white, Anglo-Saxon, and Protestant, he was your neighbor. If anybody wasn't, you could give him the works. You didn't have to love him.

Now, Jesus said, you had to love your neighbor, and this lawyer thought he would create a name for himself by putting Jesus on the spot. Jesus had gone around doin' a lot of preachin' to the Samaritans, and this lawyer thought, "If that guy preaches that social equality stuff right here in Jerusalem, there's gonna be enough of these red necks to really tar and feather him. We'll fix him up."

So Jesus said, "Well, Colonel, I'll tell you a little story." And here Jesus is hiding his truth. The lawyer knows he's gonna catch it, but he doesn't know how or when. He's on, and he's gotta ride; Jesus is pickin' up speed, and the lawyer can't jump off.

In the course of the story, Jesus talked first about a priest. But down south, we don't have many priests. Everybody down there is either a Methodist or a Baptist, unless somebody's been tinkering with him. So we'll call him a preacher.

As the preacher whizzed by the beaten man by the side of the road, his homiletic mind probably made the following outline: (1) I do not know the man. (2) I do not wish to get involved in any court proceedings. (3) I don't want to get blood on my new upholstery. (4) The man's lack of proper clothing would embarrass me upon my arrival in town. (5) Finally, brethren, a minister must never be late for a revival meeting. He was going to preach that evening on "God Is Love."

Next, Jesus mentioned the Levite. What is a Levite? Those folks standin' out there in front of Jesus knew what a Levite was. In those days there was the Levitical tribe, and all of the descendants of Levi were the preachers. You didn't get a call to preach then. You were born a preacher by bein' in the Levitical tribe.

But Levi had so many descendants down through the

centuries that pretty soon there were more preachers than there were pulpits. They had to find other work for these Levites to do, and they became assistant ministers. Then, when they filled up all those slots, they became ministers of music.[1] Now, this fellow perhaps was the minister of music, or maybe we'd call him the hymn leader. He was going to help in the revival songfest.

This Levite saw the injured man, but he had told the junior choir to meet him half an hour early. He wanted to teach 'em a little junior song: "Brighten the corner where you are." Besides, you can start a meetin' without a preacher, but you got to have somebody there to heist a tune.

If the preacher and the minister of music aren't going to stop, who is going to help this poor fellow? Jesus said that another traveler came along. He was driving an old Model T. They say those were the most religious automobiles ever made. They shook the devil out of more folks than any other car. I can see it now. It had a huge front end with magnesium lights. Each time the back tire went around, it would go "ahump, ahump." Its window shades were flapping in the wind.

He came churning along at about fifteen to twenty miles per hour, and he stopped. Of course, he didn't have much trouble stopping, but he stopped.

"Who could it be?" the lawyer asked. "Who was it?"

Jesus said he was a black man.[2] He got out of his car and saw this man lying there. He might have said something along this line: "Somebody's robbed you. Yeah, I know about that; I've been robbed, too. And they beat you up bad; I know, I've been beat up, too. And everybody just went right on by and left you here hurting; yeah, I know, they pass me by too."

He drove him into town and passed the revival meeting

where they were singing, "Love lifted me." Out front, their sign said, "EVERYBODY WELCOME," but the black man knew better. He took the injured fellow to the hospital, paid as much as he could toward his bill, and promised to return and pay whatever was necessary.

Jesus turned to the lawyer and said to him, "Would you tell me, please, who was the neighbor?"

This lawyer, unwilling even to say the word, drew his robes of righteousness about him and said, "Well, I, I suppose . . . I suppose it was that guy who showed mercy."

Jesus said, "You got it right. Now you go and start living that way yourself."

Now *we* have to get going and start living that way. To be merciful means to do whatever helping the situation demands, to pay whatever the poor man owes. We like to figure out in advance what we have to give up. What is mercy going to cost us? But true mercy doesn't ask for limits; it only asks for opportunity. There are no outer limits to discipleship.

We have already crossed the bridge of total dispossession when we entered the kingdom. It only remains for us now to flesh out our servanthood. It is too late to ask questions about whether we really want to die or not.

If you want to know whether mercy is actually the currency of the kingdom, then you must do it.[3] Mercy is spontaneous, not planned. There is no time for calculating possible risk or effect. What does it matter if, in the process of helping the victim beside the road, you yourself become a victim? If you are robbed and slain, then you only receive the greater opportunity to be a child of your Father, whose Son was also robbed and slain when he stopped by you in your distress.

Mercy is not traditional, not token, and not sterile. *Mercy is the creative risk of unlimited involvement.* Mercy seldom gets off the ground when we approach it from the standpoint of a hypothetical question. It begins when we see our world as a world of neighbors. It culminates when we act toward the person in need as if that person were actually Christ. This is the thrust of the parable of the last judgment.

> When the Son of Man starts his revolution with all his band around him, then he will assume authority. And all the nations will be assembled before him, and he will sort them out, like a farmer separating his cows from his hogs, penning the cows on the right and the hogs on the left.
>
> Then the Leader of the Movement will say to those on his right, "Come, you pride of my Father, share in the Movement that was set up for you since creation; for I was hungry and you shared your food with me; I was thirsty and you shared your water with me; I was a stranger and you welcomed me, ragged and you clothed me, sick and you nursed me; I was in jail, and you stood by me."
>
> Then the people of justice will answer, "Sir, when did we see you hungry and share our food, or thirsty and share our water? When did we see you a stranger and welcome you, or ragged and clothe you? When did we see you sick or in jail, and stand by you?"
>
> And the Leader of the Movement will reply,

"When you did it to one of these humblest brothers and sisters of mine, you did it to me."

Then he will say to those on his left, "Get away from me, you fallen skunks, and into the flaming hell reserved for the Confuser and his crowd. For I was hungry and you shared nothing with me; I was thirsty and you gave me no water; I was a stranger and you didn't welcome me, ragged and you didn't clothe me, sick and in jail, and you didn't stand by me."

Then these too will ask, "Sir, when did we see you hungry or thirsty or a stranger or ragged or sick or in jail, and do nothing about your needs?" Then he'll answer, "When you failed one of these humblest people, you failed me." These will take an awful beating, while the just ones will have the joy of living. (Matt. 25:31-46)

When Jesus said to those on his right, "Come, you pride of my Father, share in the Movement that was set up for you since creation," he was saying, "This revolution is not a fad. The kingdom has its roots in eternity, and it has been growing and sprouting for a long time. You all come in and enter into it."

I think Jesus was talkin' about *now* rather than future. The kingdom is a *contemporary* life of compassion, sharing, serving, identification, and empathy. He said, "I was hungry and you fed me," and they said, "When did we see you?" They didn't say, "Yes, Lord, I got that here somewhere. I sent that in with the last annual report. Let's see, oh, yeah, 219 gallons of water, 300 gallons of milk. That's pretty good, isn't it Lord? Right nice."

"I was sick and you came unto me."

"Yeah, I had to make a few phone calls, and I got that here: 3,019 phone calls; that's pretty good."

You know, we'd have it all codified, ready to send in. But these people on the right-hand side had made it such a habit that they were no longer able to keep records. Paul, in his great song of love in 1 Corinthians 13—I forget how it is in the ordinary English—but in the cotton-pickin' kind, he said, "Love keeps no books."

I think this is what Jesus was talking about. These people have risen above being statistical Christians. If you're still in the bookkeeping business, you'd better reexamine your love. You're a child; you're dealing with childish things.

He said to these people, "I expect from my followers a kind of life that identifies them. I was thirsty, and you knew how to respond." Now this is the kind of thing the Christians, many times, seem to be so dumb about. When they see a man who's thirsty, they haven't got sense enough to give him water. They bring him a hymnal.

To take an even more ridiculous example, a Baptist church I know installed a $25,000 fountain on its front lawn. That thing has the capacity of spouting a thousand gallons a minute! That's enough water for any Baptist. A thousand gallons a minute! We Baptists don't do things halfway. The people come, and Jesus says, "I was thirsty." "Yeah, Lord, and we built you a circulatin' fountain."

Now, imagine spendin' $25,000 of God Almighty's good money to put up a circulatin' fountain when some people don't even have runnin' water in their kitchens! Can you imagine people being that idiotic?

Jesus expects Christians to know how to respond. "I was thirsty, and you gave me water. I was hungry, and you gave me a dissertation on the fifth horse in the book of Revelation." Christians gotta know, it seems to me, that a hungry man gotta have bread, a thirsty man gotta have water, and a sick man gotta have a doctor, and a man in jail gotta have somebody to come to him.

I was preachin' down in Florida in February, in a rather big town down there, and I was informed that a big church had just spent $40,000 to plant a Flowers-of-the-Bible garden. They went through the Bible and found where it says "roses of Sharon." So they go to Sharon, wherever that is, and they get 'em some roses. Then they read where it says "the lilies of the valley." So they go where the valley is and get 'em some lilies.

Those people spent $40,000 on exotic plants from all over the world to make a Flowers-of-the-Bible garden so people could walk through that garden and smell the roses of Sharon and look at the lilies of the valley. I think somebody ought to put some cages up so they can have the birds of the air, especially if they'd stand under one and look up. I think that would be the most devotional experience they could have.

In that same city, I visited a daycare center with approximately seventy-five little flowers in it. They were black flowers. Their playground, I give you my word, was hardly as big as a garage. They had no equipment. And here those idiotic "Christians" spent $40,000 on exotic flowers and not one dime for God's little flowers. Can you imagine it?

So I said to the people that I was preachin' to, "You all have been complainin' to me all week about how ineffective the church is and how dead religion is. I want to make you a proposition. As soon as this thing is over, all of you get your grubbin' tools, and we'll go up there and grub up that Flowers-of-the-Bible garden, and I think we'll have a little excitement goin' on as a protest of people being so blind as to spend God Almighty's money in that way."

I couldn't find a soul who was interested in grubbing. And I didn't grub either. I've been ashamed of it ever since.

We have seen that mercy is not a program that we devise while we're praying or meditating or reading the Bible. It is an action that we take while we're walking the road. Mercy is *now*, not a future point or a five-year plan.

In the last part of this excerpt from Clarence, we can see that the demand for justice is likewise occasioned by experience rather than by analysis. We need to keep our eyes open, to listen for the sounds of human anguish, to go slow enough to stop wherever a work of mercy waits for us so that we can take the opportunity to carry out the compassion of God.

If we follow that work of mercy to conclusion, we will often be led into the yelling and pounding and nagging dimension of justice. The serious implementation of mercy creates a strong solidarity among ourselves, Jesus, and the oppressed. Among the seventy-five "little flowers" at the daycare center, we see ourselves and, more significantly, we see our Lord.

We hunger and thirst for justice to the extent that we become the victims of injustice. Clarence "couldn't find a soul who was interested in grubbing" because he couldn't find a soul who was seriously interested in mercy.

What would have happened if the good Samaritan, the black man in the Cotton Patch Version, had taken his unconscious friend to the hospital and found the attendant asleep and the doors locked? He would have done what justice required, even as he had already begun to do what mercy required.

The world has always respected and honored "good" people, because "good" people always work for change from within the system. By their participation, they unconsciously endorse the acceptability of the world order and legitimize its processes. The world order sees these "good" people as friends. But the kingdom of God stands as a witness against the world order. And the mercy and justice of God spell the end of this world's way of doing things.

Our culture has been able to immunize itself against the church by forging an unholy alliance with it. But the powers of this world can never appease the foolishness of the family of God. The children of the Father trade with the idea that to lose one's life in the works of mercy and justice is to gain one's life. It is a dangerous idea, and it makes us dangerous people: Christians on the loose!

So the parables have had to lead us, kicking and screaming perhaps, out of an old way of life into a new set of values and relationships. We have little in common with "good" people; mercy has little in common with humanitarianism; justice has little in common with reform.

We go beyond goodness to actually laying down our lives. We do not want a reshuffling of the cards. We want to start playing with a totally new deck—living-dying a totally new life—because the old cards are marked against the purposes of God no matter how they're shuffled.

12
The Parabolic Life

If we seek the kingdom, we seek justice; if we love God, we love our neighbor. If we seek justice, we are merciful, planting seeds of mercy, and we resist injustice, where structures of oppression prevent the exercise of mercy. When we love our neighbor, we become our neighbor's servant. Here we have the interlocking pieces of discipleship: justice and mercy, servanthood and resistance.

The grace of the Father reshapes our lives. Our attitude toward God becomes thanksgiving. Our understanding of ourselves becomes humility. Our response to our brothers and sisters is from the posture of servanthood: we incarnate and convey to them God's mercy. And our approach to the ideology of oppression is resistance: we raise a witness against the culture of militarism, greed, and prejudice.

How do we raise this witness? The final concern of this book is to help us put the teachings of the parables into the context of a parabolic life. Jesus not only taught in parables; he *lived* a parable. To witness for mercy and justice is more than a matter of words; it is also more than a matter of individual deeds. It is a matter of our life situation.

Jesus spoke about loving one another, sometimes in parables and sometimes in straight teaching. Jesus also performed many acts of love. But what was Jesus' life all about at its deepest level? Did his ministry consist only of the stories he told, the lives he changed, the sins he forgave, the diseases he healed, the tables he overturned? No. It was much more.

When we see Jesus' ministry as only a series of teachings and accomplishments, we count it as frustrated—

• by the nine lepers who didn't return to give thanks;[1]

• by the money changers who renewed their temple trade after Jesus had thrown them out;[2]

• by Lazarus, who was raised from the dead only to die again;[3] and

• by the world, which continues to live as if there is no God.

Jesus' outward ministry was powerful despite the real frustrations it encountered. But the wineskin of his parabolic life was surrounding this new wine of his word and deed.

> He also gave them this comparison: "No housewife ever uses new, unshrunk material to patch an old dress. If she does, the new will shrink and pull, and won't match the old material. And nobody ever puts new, fermenting wine in brittle, plastic bottles. If he does, the new will pop the old bottles, and the wine will be wasted and the bottles ruined. But new wine is put into new, strong bottles." (Luke 5:36-38)

The most tragic mistake we could make now would be to miss the point of this parable. The parables have been instilling new ideas within us. And we are trading with these ideas. But the ferment that is created by discipleship is too much for us to contain in our old life. We are like old and brittle plastic bottles.

How can we become new so that who we are fits what we say and what we do? What is the context out of which we show mercy and work for justice? We do such deeds in the context of this world. But there is a more immediate life situation over which we have control. Our own life setting unifies and flavors our ministry. It says something more powerful and more lasting than all of our separate words and deeds.

I vividly remember the Attica prison revolt in New York State in 1971. I saw a magazine account that was filled with brutal pictures. There were photos of prisoners holding knives to the necks of their hostages and of helmeted grim-faced troops ready for the command to storm the cellblock. There was a picture of several weary and rumpled officials trying to decide how to handle the uprising. Then there were the aftermath scenes of death and destruction.

In the midst of all this chaos and violence, there was a single photo of a man in a pinstriped suit, holding a press conference in an air-conditioned room miles away. He appeared to be well-rested, well-scrubbed, and well-fed. He was speaking in precise words to men and women sitting in neat rows on cushioned chairs. And he was telling them what happened at Attica.

The speaker was trying to convey the anguish of the story, complete with governmental recommendations on how to avoid future uprisings. But his lifestyle at that moment showed that he had not been personally involved. If there is any truth to the idea that the medium is message, then his message was irrelevant.

We cannot talk of the kingdom of God if our lives symbolize the kingdom of this world. We may not talk in sterile proper terms of the cost of discipleship. There must be integrity between what we do and say—the new wine—and who we are—the new wineskin.

John the Baptist was such a good symbol of repentance that he didn't need to say much. Here comes this wild-eyed radical storming out of the desert, half-naked and half-starved, telling us we have to break with our old way of life. People understood what he meant because they saw him as a living message.

John's dress and diet were not a gimmick he contrived to get people's attention. Nor were they the subjects of his preaching. He did not try to impose his lifestyle upon others. His lifestyle was a natural accompaniment for his message. So if we want to get a handle on lifestyle—the medium—we need to look again at our message.

Like Jesus, we represent the kingdom God *over against* the kingdom of this world. *If there is no "over against," there is no kingdom of God.* We should not expect our lifestyle, in its totality, to reflect what is acceptable to this world, nor should it merely reflect the neutral ground that the two kingdoms have in common.

Nevertheless, there are times when our mutual purposes permit us to cooperate with our culture. We do our best to live at peace with all,[4] and we submit ourselves to the legitimate authority of the state. But the salt loses its taste when our peaceful coexistence with the world swallows up our resistance to the world.

The preaching of the gospel includes much to which the world says "Amen." But the preaching of the gospel will eventually make you an outcast, lead you to prison, or force you underground. The kingdom of God invades and destroys the world by replacing systems of death and fear with justice and mercy.

When Jesus taught, he spoke about a new order of the Spirit. When he healed, he gave an illustration of the abundant sufficiency of the new order. And when he went to the cross, he acknowledged the absolute hostility between the old and the new.

The cross is the new wineskin. It is the inevitable culmination of the ministry of mercy and justice. It is the lifestyle of the kingdom of God as it exists within an alien culture. The cross represents the poverty of Jesus—the loss of his possessions, his friends, and his life. It represents the nonviolent subversion of the world order.

The parabolic life is a life of eventual destitution and imprisonment. Do you suppose you can be extravagant in your mercy without becoming poor? Do you suppose you can yell and pound and nag forever in demanding justice for the oppressed without society eventually plotting how to get rid of you? If you compromise your way around the dispossession and alienation that the world imposes upon the children of grace, then you neutralize your works of mercy. The wine is wasted.

We have moved now from the parables Jesus spoke to the parable that Jesus lived. The word "parable" comes from two Greek words meaning "alongside" and "to cast." A parable is a story or a life that is along-

side something else, to highlight a specific point of
similarity or distinction, to make a comparison.
Parables build bridges of enlightenment between the
known and the unknown.

Thus when Jesus told of the farmer who left the
ninety-nine "found" sheep and sought the lost sheep,
he was building a bridge between the farmer's action
and the similar action of the heavenly Father. When
Jesus took the parable of the widow and the judge and
threw it down alongside the social order of his day, he
was revealing to us the world's reluctant concern for
justice and the need for aggressive response to such
callousness.

Jesus cast his broken life alongside the wholeness of
the kingdom of God; thus he provided a sharp visual
contrast between the spiritual abundance and security
of this kingdom, and the emptiness of the kingdom of
the world. When you analyze the joy of Jesus, you are
driven to the conclusion that his joy came from doing
the will of the Father.[5]

His strength could only have come from his Mother
and Father God. His forgiveness was divine. There was
no earthly rationale for his compassion. He wasn't out
to win votes or solicit funds. There were no hidden
agendas, no strings attached.

It was as if Jesus began by saying, "Blessed are the
poor." Then he demonstrated what he meant. He said,
"Blessed are the meek." Then his life defined the term.
He told us that the last would he first, and we mar-
veled at his words. Then he became last, and we
beheld his glory. He *became* his message.

God cannot allow our witness to the kingdom to be

blurred. People need to see us as symbols of a new humanity. When we say that we are citizens of the kingdom of God, we need to make that visible. If we choose the wineskin of a comfortable and secure life, we not only raise serious questions about our level of compassion; we also hide our light under a bushel.

If for no other reason than for clarity, we ought to renounce our citizenship in this world. I believe there also are other reasons for doing so. We must avoid conflict of interest and the appearance of conflict of interest.

If we are benefiting from a cozy relationship with the status quo in terms of position, wealth, or power, then we can't really speak as representatives of God's new world order. If we say that the joy of our fellowship with Christ is sufficient for us, then he ought to be our only source of joy. If we sing, "He's all I need," then he should be all we have. We show that we believe in the promise of God when we put ourselves in that place where we have nothing to hold onto except for the promise of God.

Instead of trying to avoid the cross, we ought to welcome it. It is the best parable we have of the inherently hostile relationship that exists between the kingdom of God and the principalities and powers that rule our world. Our lives must in some ongoing creative way raise a clear witness to this hostility. If that doesn't happen, mercy and justice are removed from their redemptive context.

Keep your eye peeled for fake preachers, who come to you with sheepskins from wolf-schools.

You'll be able to distinguish them by the way they live. You know, you don't gather pecans from a persimmon tree nor peaches from a chinaberry, do you? So it is, a cultivated tree makes cultivated fruit, and a wild tree makes wild fruit. It is impossible for a cultivated tree to bear wild fruit, or for a wild tree to bear cultivated fruit. Any tree that does not produce cultivated fruit is chopped down and thrown into the fire. That's why I told you that you could know them by way they *live*.

Not everyone who glibly calls me "Lord, Lord" shall enter the God Movement, but the one who does the will of my spiritual Father. The time will come when many people will gather around and say, "L-o-ord, O L-o-ord, *we* sure did preach in your name, didn't we? And in your name *we* gave the devil a run for his money, didn't we? *We* did all kinds of stunts in your name, didn't we?" Then I'll admit right in front of everybody, "I've never known you. Get away from me, you wicked religious racketeers."

That's why the one who hears these words of mine and acts on them shall be like a wise man who built his house on the rock. Down came the rain, up rose the floods, out lashed the winds. They all cut at that house, but it didn't fall. It was on *rock* foundation.

And the one who hears these words of mine and fails to act on them shall be like an idiot who built his house on the sand. The rain came down, the floods rose up, the winds lashed out. They all cut at that house, and it fell! And my, what a collapse! (Matt. 7:15-27)

Who are the "fake preachers"? They are those who preach the gospel out of context. They talk about the good news and the changed life, but their own lives show that the demands of God allow for conformity to old allegiance.

Who are the ones who say "Lord, Lord"? They are not pagans. They are "Christians"—Christians who do the works that normally demonstrate the power of the kingdom God. But mercy has become a "stunt." Justice has been absorbed into the normal flow of cultural event. The status quo hasn't been shattered. The peace hasn't been disturbed. There has been no "over against." And the kingdom hasn't come.

Who are the "wise" ones who build their houses upon the rock? They are the ones who have put God's ideas into action, and who have surrounded those ideas with a parabolic life. Through its servanthood and resistance, the parabolic life points out that things are not as they should be. And a foretaste of a new emerging world is provided.

God "knows" us when we enter God's family, not when we are content with a superficial imitation of that family's traits. The parables have given us at best some passing entertainment, and at worst a rough ride that is happily ended, *unless* we build our homes upon the truth.

Perhaps we have listened, and listened some more, without catching on. But if our eyes have seen, and our ears have heard, and our hearts have understood, then we have been turned around.[6] The parables have led us into the kingdom of God; our lives become a fresh incarnation of God's loving and merciful character.

Notes

Author's Preface

1. The story of Clarence Jordan and the Koinonia Farm experiment is recorded in *The Cotton Patch Evidence*, by Dallas Lee (New York: Harper & Row, 1971); and *Cotton Patch for the Kingdom*, by Ann Louise Coble (Scottdale, Pa.: Herald Press, 2001). Also see www.koinoniapartners.org.

2. Dallas Lee, ed., *The Substance of Faith and Other Cotton Patch Sermons* (New York: Association Press, 1971).

Introduction

1. Dorothy Kalins, *Cutting Loose: A Civilized Guide for Getting Out of the System* (New York: Saturday Review Press, 1973).

2. Overcoming Old Allegiance

1. Clarence called the parables *comparisons* because they compared an aspect of common experience with an otherwise obscure aspect of spiritual truth.

2. Isa. 6:9-10.

3. Reaching Out for Liberation

1. It is significant that the Greek word for "judgment" is *krisis*, from which comes our English word *crisis*.

2. John 8:32.

3. Matt. 21:45-46; Luke 20:19.

4. This translation is one that Clarence made directly from the Greek text during a talk. It is not identical to his published Cotton Patch Version.

5. Luke 13:30; Matt. 19:30; 20:16; Mark 10:31. Cf. Luke 14:11; 18:14; Matt. 23:12.

6. To be literate and able to buy or borrow books is strong circumstantial evidence that one is "on top."

7. See 2 Sam. 11:1—12:15.

8. Mark 6:17-18.

9. Based on 2 Sam. 11—12.

10. Ps. 51.

4. God Against the Church!

1. I agree with Clarence that not all people are actually children of God and therefore not all are actually brothers and sisters, even though they should be and could be. Nevertheless, at other places in this book, I will refer to our "brothers and sisters," meaning all of our fellow humans. I do not intend to blur the distinction between the actual and the ideal, but only to reinforce the intention that God has for us. We should not call ourselves "brothers and sisters" when there is great disparity between the circumstances of our lives. But we need to see ourselves as brothers and sisters in order to be reconciled to each other and God.

2. Here Jordan used a term others had often called him and the people of Koinonia: "nigger-lovers."

3. Matt. 5:44-45; Luke 6:27, 35.

4. Some homes in the Holy Land had animals on a lower level, with room above for the family.

5. In the original Cotton Patch Version, Clarence refers to the Greek word *drachma* as a "dime." I have changed it to "penny" to make the translation conform to the commentary that he gave at a later time. Perhaps we can credit the difference to inflation!

6. "Healthy people don't need a doctor—only the sick do. I haven't come to challenge the 'saved' people to a new way of walking—only the 'sinners'" (Luke 5:31-32).

7. It was undoubtedly offensive to Jesus' hearers, as it may be to us, that God is portrayed as a woman.

8. Luke 4:16-30.

9. This is actually the modern-day equivalent of what Jesus did say. If you are a member of such a church, your response to Jesus' statement may be like the response of the Nazareth congregation.

10. Luke 19:47.

5. God Against the Rich!

1. This commentary on the rich farmer is taken from the record, "The Great Banquet and Other Parables," retold by Clarence Jordan and produced by Koinonia Records.

2. Both words carry a similar onomatopoeic sound (vocal imitation of an action): *ptuoh* meaning "I spit," and *ptohchos,* meaning "poor/beggar, spit-upon one."

6. Disturbing the Peace

1. "Yahweh, who does what is right, is always on the side of the oppressed" (Ps. 103:6, JB).

2. The term "third world" normally refers to underdeveloped nations of Africa, Asia, and Latin America. It may, as here, refer to impoverished people anywhere.

3. In the Greek, the word for "rock" is *petra*. Jesus, as Clarence's translation remembers, gave Simon the nickname "Rock" or "Peter" (Matt. 16:18).

4. In the above Cotton Patch Version, I have altered Clarence's use of personal pronouns to more accurately reflect the substance and intent of the Greek text.

5. In Romans 13, Paul develops this idea of the state as God's agent for the ordering of society along just lines. The nation as God's instrument for justice is to that extent "instituted by God" (Rom. 13:1, NRSV).

6. As we shall discuss later, the state may decide to get rid of us in a more unpleasant manner. After Jesus created a ruckus in the temple, the state and religious authorities conspired together to destroy him (Luke 19:45-48).

7. Mic. 6:6-8; Matt. 9:13.

7. Children of Arrogance

1. As popularized by John Milton in *Paradise Lost* (1667); cf. Matt. 9:34; Luke 10:18; John 12:31; 16:11.

2. Gen. 3:1-7; see NRSV note for 3:5, "like gods."

3. The "church member" and the "unsaved man" of the Cotton Patch Version are the "Pharisee" and the "publican" of the Greek text. In this commentary, taken from *The Substance of Faith*, 139-40, Clarence reverts to the literal terminology.

4. Luke 3:8.

8. Children of Grace

1. Luke 15:2 speaks literally of "the Pharisees and the scribes."

2. Luke 5:31-32 and parallels.

3. I have altered Clarence's use of personal pronouns to more accurately reflect the Greek text.

4. Some Jews, who had toiled through the heat of the day, apparently resented Jesus' extension of mercy to the Gentiles, who had not suffered with the agonies of Israel through the centuries.

5. In this passage from Luke, Jesus is again lashing out at the

propriety and timidity that keep us from entering the kingdom.

9. Counting the Cost

1. Matt. 1:23.
2. Paul said, "I live every day on death row" (1 Cor. 15:31).
3. Phil. 2:5-8.

10. Trade with These Ideas

1. The Cotton Patch Version uses sums of money to symbolize the investment that Jesus, the businessman in the parable, has made in his "assistants." In the Greek, a "talent" refers to a large amount of money, what a laborer might earn during fifteen years.

2. See parallels in Matt. 13:31-32; Mark 4:31-32. The mustard seed was the smallest known in Palestine.

3. Rev. 22:2.
4. Matt. 5:11-12.
5. Luke 11:9-10.
6. Amos 5:24.
7. Col. 3:1-17; John 1:12-13.
8. Matt. 5:13-16.
9. The Cotton Patch version, adapted to inclusive language.
10. Phil. 3:10, JB.

11. The Works of Mercy

1. See 1 Chron. 9:33.

2. Literally, he was a Samaritan. In Jesus' day, the Samaritans and the Jews often discriminated against each other because they were of different ancestry and religious backgrounds, though both honored the books of Moses.

3. Jesus said that God would confirm his will to us while we were in the process of carrying it out; John 7:17.

12. The Parabolic Life

1. Luke 17:12-19.

2. Matt. 21:12-17. Jesus' defiant act did not mark the end of the rich exploiting the poor in the name of religion.

3. John 11:1-44.
4. Heb. 12:14.
5. Ps. 40:8; Heb. 10:5-7.
6. See Matt. 13:13-17.

The Authors

Florence and Clarence Jordan in 1959. Courtesy of Hargrett Rare Book and Manuscript Library, University of Georgia

Clarence Jordan is widely known for his Cotton Patch Version of the New Testament and as founder of Koinonia, an interracial farming community at Americus, Georgia.

Recognized as a compelling and dramatic speaker, Jordan addressed many church conferences and conventions. He died on October 29, 1969, while preparing a speech to deliver the next day at Mercer University, Macon, Georgia.

Born to a prominent family in Talbotton, Georgia, Jordan held a B.S. degree in agriculture from the University of Georgia, and Th.M. and Ph.D. degrees in New Testament Greek from Southern Baptist Theological Seminary, Louisville, Kentucky.

At that seminary in 1933, Clarence met his wife-to-be, Florence Kroeger. They had four children: Eleanor,

James Frederick, Janet Elizabeth, and Frank Leonard. In 1942 the Jordans and the Martin and Mabel England family moved onto the Georgia farm where they began the Koinonia ministry. Florence died on June 17, 1987.

Jordan's published works include the following: *The Cotton Patch Version of Matthew and John, The Cotton Patch Version of Luke and Acts, The Cotton Patch Version of Paul's Epistles, The Cotton Patch Version of Hebrews and the General Epistles,* and *The Substance of Faith and Other Cotton Patch Sermons* (all by Association Press), and *Sermon on the Mount* (Judson Press).

Various records and cassettes from Clarence Jordan's speaking are available from Koinonia Partners, Route 2, Americus, GA 31709.

Bill Lane Doulos became a friend of Koinonia when he first visited in 1970. He is a former member of their board of directors.

Bill spent three years as a staff instructor for Young Life Campaign in Pittsburgh before finishing his Master of Divinity degree at Fuller Theological Seminary in Pasadena, California.

At the time, he was a Presbyterian and had been considering ordination to the ministry. But by the time he received his degree, in 1974, he had wandered a block west of Fuller to an Episcopal parish called All Saints.

Bill began attending a Rock Mass at All Saints once a month, partly in protest of the United States' involvement in the Vietnam War. Then he became a volunteer at a social service outreach that the church sponsored called Union Station.

Upon graduating from Fuller, Bill joined the staff at All Saints, with responsibility for urban social work. He invested most of his time with Union Station until he retired as its Executive Director in 1990.

By then he had already ventured to the skid-row district of Los Angeles, where he managed two hotels on behalf of another nonprofit, the Church and Temple Housing Corporation. Seeking affordable housing for the poor became a natural extension of his work at Union Station.

Today Bill continues his urban social and pastoral work for All Saints as a lay eucharistic minister, while he directs a relatively new nonprofit called Jubilee Enterprises. Jubilee operates sober-living communities for about a hundred residents in the Pasadena area, working with the formerly homeless, imprisoned, and addicted.

Bill was born William Henry Lane II in Johnstown, Pennsylvania, in 1943. Three booklets published under Bill's former name are available from Koinonia: *The Christian and Materialism, The Radical Church,* and *The Christian Radical.* In addition to this volume, he has authored two other books: *A Journey of Compassion: Letters from a Street Minister,* and *Hearts on Fire: The Evolution of an Urban Church.*